Religion and Law in South Africa

Religion and Law in South Africa

Charles Maimela

This book was originally published as a monograph in the International Encyclopaedia of Laws/Religion.

Founding Editor: Roger Blanpain
General Editor: Frank Hendrickx
Volume Editor: Rik Torfs

Wolters Kluwer

Published by:
Kluwer Law International B.V.
PO Box 316
2400 AH Alphen aan den Rijn
The Netherlands
E-mail: international-sales@wolterskluwer.com
Website: lrus.wolterskluwer.com

Sold and distributed in North, Central and South America by:
Wolters Kluwer Legal & Regulatory U.S.
7201 McKinney Circle
Frederick, MD 21704
United States of America
Email: customer.service@wolterskluwer.com

Sold and distributed in all other countries by:
Air Business Subscriptions
Rockwood House
Haywards Heath
West Sussex
RH16 3DH
United Kingdom
Email: international-customerservice@wolterskluwer.com

Printed on acid-free paper

ISBN 978-94-035-1151-1

e-Book: ISBN 978-94-035-1200-6
web-PDF: ISBN 978-94-035-1201-3

Printed in the United Kingdom.

The Author

Charles Maimela is a Senior Lecturer in the Department of Private Law at the University of Pretoria, South Africa. Dr Maimela teaches Legal Pluralism, Law of Damages and Law of Delicts to law students. He holds the following qualifications: LLB (Unisa), LLM (Unisa) and LLD (Unisa).

The Author

Table of Contents

List of Abbreviations

ACHPR	African Court on Human and Peoples' Rights
AIDS	Acquired Immune Deficiency Syndrome
ANC	African National Congress
APRM	African Peer Review Mechanism
AQIM	Al Qaeda of the Islamic Maghreb
AU	African Union
BCEA	Basic Conditions of Employment Act
CCMA	Commission for Conciliation, Mediation & Arbitration
COIDA	Compensation for Occupational Injuries and Diseases Act
CRL	Cultural, Religious and Linguistic Communities
DA	Democratic Alliance
EU	European Union
EEA	Employment Equity Act
HIV	Human Immunodeficiency Virus
HPCSA	Health Professions Council of South Africa
ICCPR	International Covenant on Civil and Political Rights
ICC	International Criminal Court
ICESCR	International Covenant on Economic, Social and Cultural Rights
ICJ	International Court of Justice
ICTY	International Criminal Tribunal for the former Yugoslavia
IMF	International Monetary Fund
JSC	Judicial Services Commission

List of Abbreviations

LAC	Labour Appeals Court
L&D	Laws and Disciplines (of the Methodist Church of Southern Africa)
LRA	Labour Relations Act
NPA	National Prosecuting Authority
NGOs	Non-governmental Organisations
NEPAD	New Partnership for Africa's Development
OHSA	Occupational Health and Safety Act
OAU	Organisation for African Unity
PAC	Pan African Movement
PCIJ	Permanent Court of International Justice
SADC	Southern African Development Community
SDA	Skills Development Act
TAC	Treatment Action Campaign
TRC	Truth and Reconciliation Commission
UDHR	Universal Declaration of Human Rights
UNESCO	United Nations Educational, Scientific and Cultural Organisation
UIA	Unemployment Insurance Act
UN	United Nations

General Introduction

§1. General Background of the Country

I. Geographical Background

1. South Africa is located in the southern part of the African continent. It comprises of nine provinces: Gauteng, Limpopo, Northern Cape, Western Cape, North West Free State; KwaZulu-Natal; Mpumalanga and Eastern Cape. The geographical position of South Africa is considered to be perfect because it is the producer of important minerals which include gold and diamonds among other natural resources.[1] This has resulted in making South Africa one of the leading economically developed states in the African continent.[2] Each province among the nine provinces of South Africa is unique and contributes to the overall vision and mission of making South Africa a dynamic and sound country in the African continent. For example, Gauteng province is the smallest province in South Africa and overly populated. This is attributed to the fact that most mining industries and economic activities of South Africa are vested in this province.[3] Based on this economic position of Gauteng it attracts people from all walks of life, particularly from different African countries and locals from other provinces in pursuit of wealth and better opportunities. This means that the people who reside in this province are diverse and share one common goal of making a better living.[4]

2. The province of Gauteng despite its mining and industrial activity is also known for big cities like Pretoria, which is the seat of government and the capital city of South Africa, and Johannesburg, which is the city that is regarded as the economic hub of South Africa because it is an industrial city and has the richest square mill which is Sandton city among other things.[5] The Limpopo province is one of the rural provinces of South Africa and contributes with regard to farming activities for the country and most of the people from this province move to Gauteng in search

1. B. Buscher, The *Political Economy of Africa's Natural Resources and the Great Financial Crisis*, 26 TESG 137 (2011).
2. *Ibid.*, at 138.
3. C. Fourie, *Why Is Johannesburg the Economic Hub of South Africa: A City of Opportunities for Entrepreneurs*, 3 Randburg Sun 4 (2017).
4. *Ibid.*
5. *Ibid.*

of better opportunities.[6] Western Cape is also one of the developed and economically sound provinces in South Africa. This is due to the fact that Table Mountain and Ocean in the city of Cape Town serve as a major boost to the tourism of the country. Cape Town is a well-known and regarded city across the world due to its beauty and Mediterranean climate. The Western Cape province experiences Mediterranean climate, which means that it experiences rain in winter season; however this is not the case for the other eight provinces of South Africa.[7] Furthermore, the Western Cape also plays a major role when it comes to food production and security through grape and apple farms as well as the production of tea such as Rooibos. In turn, this results in the production of wines and juices, which are well known in the world, and are considered for both imports and exports purposes in the country and beyond.[8]The Northern Cape is the largest province in South Africa and boasts of agricultural land and also various solar systems that are well known, for example, in connection with detecting weather conditions for the rest of the country.[9]

3. North West province is regarded as the platinum province because it is the world producer of platinum. It is also known for its rich soil for farming, and it plays a role in food production in the country, in particular vegetables and other staple foods.[10] The province of Mpumalanga, which means where the sun rises, is one of the provinces that is leading in coal mining and production. Tourism is also one of the strong factors which is dominating in this province. Mpumalanga prides itself as being home to the Kruger National Park, which is the biggest game reserve in the African continent, and consists of big fives (the Lion, Leopard, Buffalo, Elephant and Rhino) as the official residents of the park.[11]

4. KwaZulu-Natal is the warmest and friendly province in South Africa, and it is put on the map by the city of Durban for its beautiful and clean beaches as well as hotels and resorts, which are favourites among both locals and international visitors. However, tourism is not the only factor or blueprint that determines this province; this is because this province is the largest sugar producer due to the sugar plantations that rest on the belly of this province. This means that this province contributes for the economy of South Africa through sugar production and tourism.[12]

---

6. *The Great Limpopo Province, History of the Province*, http://www.dolimpopo.com/limpopo-province (accessed 6 Jul. 2018).
7. P. De Lille, *The Western Cape Government: History and Regional Development Profile for the City of Cape Town* 3 WCG 14 (2018).
8. Cape Town is also a city which hosts parliament where law is made and where the executive, which is the government, is called to account from the various political parties that are represented in parliament. *See* De Lille, *supra* n. 3 at 15.
9. J. Morris, *Northern Province and the Karoo Rock in South Africa*, 55 Journal of Human Evolution 11 (2016).
10. J. Nkosi *Investment Potential of the Platinum Province: Areas of Investment That Are Expected to Grow Fast Include Fuel Cell Technology, Machinery for Mining, Energy Manufacturing and Component Production*, 4 Global Africa 12 (2017).
11. *Mpumalanga and the Big Five Animals*, https://www.mpumalanga-info.co.za/provinces/article/378/big-five-animals-in-south-africa (accessed 17 Aug. 2018).
12. *A Warm Welcome to Kwazulu Natal in South Africa*, http://www.zulu.org.za/about/key-facts/welcome (accessed 16 Aug. 2018).

Free State province is also an active province in farming activities due to the vast land that is found in the province and is considered to be a beautiful province due to the city of Bloemfontein which is regarded as the city of roses because of the beautiful flowers which are found only in that city. This results in an increase in tourism in order to explore the beauty of this province, and there are other tourist attractions to see and enjoy for both locals and visitors.[13] Finally, the province of Eastern Cape is also one of the largest provinces second to the Northern Cape and has a rich history when it comes to the liberation of the South African community. This province is known as the home of legends, because struggle stalwarts in South Africa come from this province and this includes the well-known and regarded Nelson Mandela among others.[14] Furthermore, this province has rich agricultural land, which plays a major role when it comes to farming activities.[15]

5. Based on the geographical position or location of South Africa, it is very important to note that it is a tourist's hub and also a socio-economical country that is in a position to develop and prosper on the basis of its position. The South African economy is driven by mining and agriculture because South Africa is one of the leading exporters of raw materials like cold, coal, gold and platinum to name but a few.[16] South Africa enjoys these benefits because of its geographical location or position, which in a nutshell, it positions the country far better than other African countries, and as it is often argued or believed that indeed South Africa has been blessed and has seen the grace of God. This is due to the prosperity it enjoys and prides itself with, due to its geographical position or location. It is important for the reader to further bear in mind that each province in South Africa is unique and has a role to play with the aim of making sure that a country like South Africa becomes a world leader in terms of its economic position. One can sum up the role and position of each province in South Africa as unique with the aim of putting South Africa and the continent of Africa on the map, by ensuring that they complement and work together effectively in building the rainbow nation of South Africa.

II. Population

6. South Africa is still a developing country with a population size of about 57 million people, and this figure excludes people who have entered the country illegally or legally for different reasons as part of migration and bearing in mind the geographical location of South Africa as already discussed above.[17] The population of South Africa can best be described as pluralistic in nature, and this means that the population of South Africa is diverse. Different people from different cultural

13. F. Richardson, *The Orange Free State and Inhabitants* 5 (Cambridge University Press 11th ed. 1999).
14. *South African History Online*, www.sahistory.org.za (accessed on 5 Jun. 2018).
15. *South African History Online Place of Birth of Nelson Mandela*, www.sahistory.org.za (accessed on 5 Jun. 2018).
16. Nkosi, *supra* n. 10, at 12.
17. *Statistics of the Population of South Africa*, http://www.statssa.gov.za/publications/P0302/P030220 18.pdf (accessed 11 Jul. 2018).

and religious backgrounds make up the South African population. This is the reason why South Africa is regarded as the rainbow nation.[18] South Africa has eleven official languages: English, Afrikaans, IsiZulu, IsiXhosa, South Sotho, North Sotho, Setswana, Ndebele, Xitsonga, Tshivenda and Sepedi.[19] Out of the eleven official languages as outlined, both English and Afrikaans owe their historical roots or connection to the colonisers of South Africa. This is because South Africa was colonised by both the English and Dutch at some point and one cannot discuss the history and legal system of South Africa without referring to both the English and Dutch legal systems. The reason why both systems of English and Dutch are significant when one is discussing the position of South Africa is because the legal system of South Africa is built from both the English and Dutch legal systems, which makeup what is known as common law in South Africa.[20] This means that the systems of both English and Dutch did not only play a role in relation to languages but it played an important role when it comes to the development and shaping of the legal system of South Africa as it is known today. The other nine official languages form a part of the indigenous communities of South Africa, and the people who speak these languages are spread out across the nine provinces of South Africa and majority are black Africans.[21] However, it is important to bear in mind that because the South African community or population is pluralistic it does not mean that only black Africans are allowed to speak these indigenous languages. People from other ethnic groups like white Africans, for example, are not barred from speaking them, but they are encouraged to do so as part of nation building.[22] This is because freedom of association and expression is protected in the Constitution in terms of section 16 of the Constitution of the Republic of South Africa, 1996 (herewith referred to as the Constitution).[23]

7. The debate currently in South Africa is based on the fact that despite the recognition of various languages, still a lot of work needs to be done to add other languages which have not been recognised thus far, even after twenty-four years of democracy. This new language is sign language, which will accommodate people living with disability, and it is argued that the incorporation of this language into the recognised languages in the Republic will be one of the progressive and socially relevant moves with the aim of ensuring that people living with disabilities are

18. J. Bekker & C. Rautenbach, *Introduction to Legal Pluralism* 12 (LexisNexis, South Africa 4th ed. 2015).
19. *Ibid.*, at 13.
20. *Ibid.*, at 14.
21. Section 6(2) of the *Constitution of the Republic of South Africa*, 1996 (herewith referred as the Constitution) provides that in recognising the historically diminished use and status of indigenous languages of our people, the state must take practical and positive measures to elevate the status and advance the use of these languages.
22. Section 6(2) of the Constitution.
23. Section 16(1) of the Constitution states that everyone has the right to freedom of expression, which includes: freedom of the press and media; freedom to receive or impart information or ideas; freedom of artistic creativity; and lastly academic freedom and freedom of scientific research.

accommodated in the South African society.[24] Without a doubt to include sign language as one of the official languages in South Africa will surely put South Africa in the world map and a leader in the African continent to such an extent that it will be seen as a country that embraces diversity even though it is diverse by its nature. Furthermore, it will be regarded as a state that cares and recognises people who suffer from disabilities and in this case particularly people who are deaf and dumb.[25]

8. The population of South Africa, which is 57 million as outlined, comprises of people from different backgrounds based on their culture and colour, but it is important to bear in mind that they all make up the South African community or society irrespective of their diversity. The population comprises of black Africans who are the original inhabitants of South Africa and are the majority in the country.[26] They are considered the custodians of the nine indigenous languages as outlined above and indigenous culture and practices.[27] White Africans owe their historical roots to the colonial past of South Africa, and they are a minority in South Africa. This ethnic group speaks both English and Afrikaans.[28] Furthermore, the South African community is made up of Indians who owe their ancestral links to Gandhi as they were brought in by the colonisers to South Africa as slaves in the sugar plantations of KwaZulu-Natal.[29] South Africa also comprises of people from Asian background who form a part of the population of South Africa and are a minority in the country.[30]

9. Based on the above assessment it is very clear that the South African community or society is diverse and pluralistic in nature. To best sum up the population of South Africa, one can say that it is multicultural in nature due to the various cultural and legal systems, which will be explored later on in this research text.

III. Government Administration

10. When it comes to the government administration in South Africa, it is a democratically elected government and the country goes to elections every five

24. T. Reagan *South African Sign Language and Language in Education Policy in South Africa*, 38 Linguistics 166 (2008).
25. People who suffer from different physical and mental deformities are often neglected in both developed and developing countries, and the incorporation of sign language can be one of the solutions to resolve and eradicate this problem encountered by the developing world. *See* Reagan, *supra* n. 24, at 167.
26. Bekker & Rautenbach, *supra* n. 18 at 20.
27. *Ibid.*
28. *Ibid.*, at 21.
29. K. Ma, *Control and Conscience: Positivist Approaches to Religion in India and South Africa*, 260 SOAS LJ 261 (2015).
30. Ma, *supra* n. 24, at 262.

years for the will of the people through free and fair elections.[31] This was unfortunately not the case in the past because during the colonial and apartheid era only white people were considered competent and eligible to vote and they enjoyed certain privileges. All of this happened at the exclusion of black people who were considered as sub-humans and were not eligible to vote, but were subject to white rule and oppression.[32] Black Africans did not have a voice in government formation and how they would want to be governed, even though they were the majority in the country, and they were the original inhabitants of South Africa. The oppression of black Africans ended in 1994 when the first election was held and the first president was democratically elected, which was the late President Nelson Mandela.[33] The reader will be taken through the process and history as to how apartheid and colonial rule were destroyed in South Africa, with religion in particular, in chapters that will follow, when discussing the role of religion in the liberation of South Africa. However, for now it is important to note that all the people of South Africa are eligible to vote and have a voice on who would govern and how they would like to be governed by their chosen government.[34] The period of 1994 is one of the foundational periods in the history of South Africa because it gave rise to the Constitution of the Republic of South Africa, which consists of a Bill of Rights that protects the fundamental rights of all people in South Africa.[35] Furthermore, multi-party democracy was and is still encouraged, and it is considered the order of the day in South Africa and in the area of politics as part of growing the young democracy of South Africa.[36]

11. From 1994 until 2018, the government of South Africa was run by the African National Congress (ANC), which was elected to power through the democratic processes of elections every five years.[37] The government of South Africa is divided into the following three tiers, which make up the government of the Republic of South Africa.[38] The national government is the first tier or branch, which comprises of the president and his or her cabinet. The second tier is the provincial government, which is run by the various premiers in the nine provinces with their respective cabinets and lastly the local government tier, which comprises of different

31. Section 1 of the Constitution states that the Republic of South Africa is one sovereign, democratic state founded on the following values: human dignity, the achievement of equality and the advancement of human rights and freedoms; non-racialism and non-sexism; Supremacy of the Constitution and the rule of law; universal adult suffrage, a national voters' roll, regular elections and a multi-party system of democratic government, to ensure accountability, responsiveness and openness.
32. Bekker & Rautenbach, *supra* n. 18, at 22.
33. J. Marrison, *Nelson Mandela, South Africa's First Black President, Dies at the Age of 95*, 5 The Washington Times 14 (2015).
34. Section 1 of the Constitution.
35. Chapter 2 of the Constitution is the Bill of Rights and it sets out the fundamental rights of all South Africans, which include the rights to human dignity and equality among other things. The Bill of Rights also make provision as to when rights can be limited.
36. Section 1 of the Constitution.
37. The ANC was formed in 1912 and it is the oldest liberation movement not only in South Africa but also in the entire continent of Africa. *See* s 1 of the Constitution.
38. Section 8 of the Constitution.

municipalities spread out across the nine provinces.[39] The local government ensures that essential services reach the people. These include water and electricity, and both the national and provincial governments respectively oversee with the aim of ensuring that people on the ground are provided with all the essential services.

12. All the three branches of government are essentially one, and this structure of division in government is aimed at ensuring that the government is close to the people and the needs of society are provided through the process of service delivery, with the much-needed urgency.

IV. Judicial Administration

13. South Africa is a constitutional democracy, section 2 of the Constitution states that the Constitution is the supreme law of the land, and any law found to be inconsistent with the Constitution must be declared null and void and the obligations imposed by it must be fulfilled.[40] This means that the rule of law is supreme in the Republic, and the government is duty bound to respect and uphold the Constitution in its function of providing services to the public, and the same can be said for the inhabitants of the Republic.

14. The Constitution as the supreme law of the land has set down mechanisms in place, which are aimed at ensuring that democracy in South Africa is protected and also maintained through the process of outlining how the state needs to function. Provision is made in the Constitution that the state for its functionality is divided into three spheres: the executive which is the government as outlined above; the legislature, which is parliament, that is responsible for the creation and formulation of laws. Furthermore, parliament is also a place where the executive is called to account in cases where they fail to execute their role towards the people of South Africa. In parliament multi-party democracy and representation is encouraged due to the diverse nature of the South African population. The judiciary, which is the last sphere of government, acts as a watchdog and ensures that the rule of law is upheld at all times. Independence of the judiciary is also protected by the Constitution to such an extent that courts are able to give decisions that do not favour the government with the aim of developing and protecting the democracy in South Africa.[41]

15. The judiciary plays a significant role in the South African democratic dispensation and justice must be accessible to all the people of South Africa irrespective of their socio-economic position, background, colour, religion or cultural beliefs. This is the reason why the structure of the judiciary through the various

39. *Ibid.*
40. Section 2 of the Constitution.
41. Section 165(2) of the Constitution states that courts are independent and subject only to the Constitution and the law, which they must apply impartially and without fear, favour or prejudice.

courts is spread out in the length and breadth of South Africa in terms of section 166 of the Constitution.[42] Section 166 of the Constitution provides for the following court structures.

A. The Constitutional Court

16. This is the highest court in the land and it deals with only constitutional matters. It is the highest court in handling constitutional matters and the highest Court of Appeal when it comes to constitutional matters. The Constitutional Court is not a Court of First Instance, meaning one cannot approach this court directly, except if one has compelling and substantive reasons to this effect.[43] This court consists of eleven justices who serve for a non-renewal term of twelve years each, and the head of this court is the chief justice who is assisted by the deputy chief justice.[44] This court currently sits in the city of Johannesburg, built in the area or vicinity of the former female prison where women lost their lives during the apartheid era. The Constitutional Court is considered the guardian of the South African democracy, and it plays an important part in the administration of justice and preservation of the hard-earned democracy of South Africa through the application and enforcement of the Constitution.

B. The Supreme Court of Appeal

17. The Supreme Court of Appeal is the highest Court of Appeal in terms of non-constitutional matters.[45] This court only listens to appeals from the various divisions of the high courts in South Africa, and the decisions it makes in such matters are considered final and binding. The head of this court is the judge president and deputy judge president and they work with other judges who are appointed by the court to ensure that the administration of justice is provided to all the people in South Africa. This court sits in the city of Bloemfontein, which is affectionately known as the city of roses, in the province of Free State.

C. The High Courts

18. High courts are spread throughout the country in each province for the administration of justice. High courts each have a judge president and deputy judge president who are responsible for the courts' administration and day-to-day operation of the courts and are assisted by the various judges who are appointed by that

42. Section 166 of the Constitution.
43. Section 167(3) of the Constitution.
44. Section 167(1) of the Constitution.
45. Section 168(3) of the Constitution.

particular division or court.[46] High courts listen to different matters, including criminal and civil matters; they also hear constitutional matters, but the final arbiter in such matters will remain the Constitutional Court as already outlined above.[47] However, it is important to note that the high court has inherent jurisdiction and is the upper guardian of all minors, and this means that this is the type of court that is vested with the best interests of minors as provided for in section 28 of the Constitution.[48]

D. Magistrate Courts

19. Magistrate courts are divided into two categories: regional courts and district courts. Regional courts have a higher jurisdiction than the district courts, and they can try a person who has been convicted with murder. Regional courts are stationed in the various major cities of South Africa, and they aim to alleviate the burden from the high courts.[49] The presiding officer in the regional courts is the chief magistrate, who will be assisted by other magistrates. In contrast to the regional courts, district courts are spread out in the townships and rural areas of South Africa.[50] The jurisdiction of the district courts is limited and the presiding officers are the chief magistrate and other magistrates who are stationed in that particular court.

E. Small Claims Court

20. Small claims court has a very limited jurisdiction, and the amount of dispute between the parties must not exceed ZAR 5,000.[51] Legal representation is not permitted in this court and only the parties of the dispute will appear before the presiding officer who is a commissioner from the ranks of advocate, attorney or legal academic.[52] The commissioners in the small claims courts are not remunerated, and they do the work as a community engagement or service with the aim of harnessing their skills as well as ensuring that the administration of justice is achieved through resolving the dispute of the parties without any delay.

F. Specialised Courts

21. In a country like South Africa with a developing democracy, litigation is increasing and the court rolls are high. The reader must bear in mind that as per the

46. Section 169 of the Constitution.
47. Section 167(3) of the Constitution.
48. Section 28 of the Constitution affirms the upper guardianship of the high court when it comes to determining the best interests of minor children.
49. Section 170 of the Constitution.
50. *Ibid.*
51. *Ibid.*
52. *Ibid.*

Constitution each and every person in South Africa has a right to fair and speedy trial, and in order to realise this right the government has set mechanisms in place to ensure that this materialises through the establishment of specialised courts.[53] Specialised courts include the Labour Court and Labour Appeals Court (LAC), which strictly listen to labour disputes between employer and employee or between a trade union and the employer.[54] Specialised commercial courts deal with offences like fraud, corruption and other white-collar crimes.[55] The minister of justice and constitutional development has powers that are vested in him by the Constitution to establish circuit courts in the various provinces to deal with, for example, divorce or any matter that the minister may deem fit with the aim of ensuring that the administration of justice is realised for all the people in South Africa as guaranteed by the Constitution.[56]

V. The Practice of Law in South Africa

22. The court structures as outlined above display how the judicial system of South Africa is structured and how it functions. However, it will be an incomplete picture if the reader is not given a brief background in relation to the role players or practitioners that appear before these various courts, as agents.

23. In South Africa for a person to be eligible to practice law and to be considered a fit and proper person, he or she must first be in possession of an LLB degree.[57] In case a person wants to be an admitted attorney, he or she must further train as a candidate attorney for two years and then write board exams after the training.[58] It is important to note that an attorney can appear in all the courts as outlined above, but must apply to be admitted to appear in the high court because attorneys are not litigation specialists.[59] In contrast to being an attorney, one can elect to be an advocate and such a person must do one year of in-house training at the bar council, which is pupillage, and write bar exams. Advocates work on briefs from attorneys and they are litigation specialists and have automatic entrance to appear in all the courts as discussed.[60] Furthermore, a candidate with an LLB degree can elect to be a prosecutor; he or she must go through the in-house training at the National Prosecuting Authority for a year, and will mostly work to prosecute criminal matters in both the high courts and magistrates courts.[61]

24. However, the practice of law in South Africa is not confined to the three career options that are outlined above; it goes further than that because a person

53. Section 35 of the Constitution.
54. Section 170 of the Constitution.
55. *Ibid.*
56. *Ibid.*
57. Section 3 of the Attorney's Act of 1979.
58. Section 4 of the Attorney's Act of 1979.
59. Section 13 of the Attorney's Act of 1979 and s. 3 of Right of Appearance in Court Act 62 of 1995.
60. Section 3 of the Advocate's Act 74 of 1964.
61. *Ibid.*

with an LLB can also choose to be an academic and embark on postgraduate studies.[62] Furthermore, one can also choose to be an adviser or researcher in the various state institutions, and this shows that the practice of law is not only confined to the courts but it is beyond that aspect. From the various courts as discussed above, it must be noted that the presiding officers in the courts are recruited from the ranks of advocates, attorneys and academics who are experienced and have been in the fraternity for a long time. Once a person is appointed as a judicial officer, they must be impartial and objective all the time with the aim of ensuring that justice is served. The judicial officers of South Africa owe their allegiance to the Constitution and the same applies to the legal practitioners. In case where a judicial officer is found to have acted inappropriately then the Judicial Service Commission (JSC), which is a body that deals with the appointment of judicial officers, will embark on an investigation and disciplinary processes on the responsible judicial official.[63] The same is the case with a legal practitioner who has abused his or her position of trust with clients. That practitioner will be disciplined by the law society in his or her area of jurisdiction or the relevant bar council.[64] These statutory bodies aim to ensure that the integrity of the legal profession is protected at all times, while ensuring that justice is administered to the people of South Africa without fear or favour.

VI. Conclusion

25. South Africa is a developing democracy with a very vibrant Constitution, which champions the fundamental rights of all people in the Republic, and this is evident from the various mechanisms it has set in place with the aim of protecting and preserving democracy. A lot still needs to be done in ensuring that the rule of law is preserved and championed in this young constitutional democracy. The next chapter will focus on the history and social aspect of South Africa with particular reference to religion, which is the main focus of this research endeavour.

§2. Social and Historical Facts About Religion in South Africa

I. Introduction

26. South Africa like all the countries in Africa did not escape the colonial rule and apartheid system. The apartheid era in South Africa can best be described as the dark period for the country due to the atrocities that were committed by the apartheid government on black people.[65] Millions of lives were lost and the degrading as well as painful oppression of the majority people by minority white people form part of this rich history of South Africa. The question the reader is probably

62. *Ibid.* and s 3 of the Attorney's Act of 1979.
63. Section 177 of the Constitution sets out the grounds on which the JSC, after it has done an investigation, can remove a judicial officer from office on the basis of gross misconduct and incapacity.
64. Section 44 of the Attorney's Act of 1979 and s. 36 of the Advocate's Act 74 of 1964.
65. Bekker & Rautenbach, *supra* n. 18 at 13.

asking is how South Africa got out from the painful past of oppression and discrimination for it to be the country that it is today, a leader in the continent of Africa. Without a doubt religion was the solution apart from other political and economic pressures that were put on the then government of South Africa. Religion kept the torch burning for the liberation of South Africa.

27. Religion was one of the instruments that were used to bring social cohesion, and it still is one of the factors that keep a pluralistic community like South Africa together to this very day. This is attributed to the fact that religion brings peace and stability without taking into account the background or colour of an individual. The diverse nature of the South African society means that different religious and cultural practices are recognised in South Africa. These include the Christian religion, Muslim religion, Hindu religion, African customary culture and practices, and all of them are recognised and are all equal as provided by the Constitution.[66]

II. The Socio-Economic Aspect of Religion in South Africa

A. During Apartheid and Colonial Period

28. Religion was one of the driving forces and instruments that have played a major role in the liberation of South Africa, with the aim of fighting the unjust practices of apartheid at the time. When looking in particular at the Christian religion there is a debate that this religion was imposed by colonisers on the South African communities and this was done through the process or work of missionaries from European countries.[67] These missionaries established independent schools in South Africa and educated the South African community in particular black children the Christian way of life. In addition, churches that preached the Christian Gospel were established in various parts of the country. Churches like the Methodist Church, Roman Catholic Church, Anglican Church, Dutch Reformed Church and Lutheran Church among others were formed due to the work of missionaries, and it is important to affirm that these churches are still functioning to this very day in South Africa.[68]

29. During this period, the South African community was educated and the doctrine of Christ formed part of their lives, particularly black people, as they were the recipients of missionary education. Despite the Christian indoctrination being introduced during the missionaries around the 1600s, still there was a great deal of oppression from the colonisers that was taking place against black people.[69] The

66. Section 15 of the Constitution states that everyone has a right to freedom of religion, conscience, thought, belief and opinion.
67. P. Coertzen, *Constitution, Charter and Religions in South Africa*, 14 AHRLJ 127 (2014).
68. *Ibid.*, at 128.
69. W.R. Kauuova, *The Religions of Southern Africa: A Synopsis of Their Basic Beliefs*, 325 Institute for Reformed Studies 3 (1997).

indigenous people of South Africa continued to suffer and receive inferior education and in most instances were denied the right to a fair and quality education. This was attributed to the fact that Afrikaans was imposed as a medium of instruction to all public schools and this was to the detriment of black people who did not understand the language.[70] This move by the apartheid government of excluding black people from mainstream educational opportunities through the use of language as a barrier and also to deny black people better opportunities of employment was unjust. This resulted in black people, particularly children, resorting to missionary schools as refuge and the redeeming feature to access better education, whose foundation, was based on the Christian way of life.[71] However, it is important to note it was not all black people who were accessing missionary education. The pupils who received missionary education were also members of that particular church that offered missionary education. This is because the foundation was largely based on the Christian methodology of that particular church formation or group.[72] The work of missionary's schools and the different church formations, which were established, played a significant role when it comes to the liberation of South Africa. This is because the liberation movement like the ANC, which is currently the governing party in South Africa, and its members were the custodians or recipients of missionary education.[73] For example, the struggle stalwart Nelson Mandela received missionary education and was a member of the Methodist Church, including other struggle stalwarts.[74]

30. These struggle stalwarts due to their Christian background and education used the church to mobilise and garner the necessary support to fight the oppressive government. This included even the various ministers of the above-mentioned church formations assisting liberation movements like the ANC and the Pan African Movement to gather at the church premises and hold secret meetings and to even provide financial means to these organisations in fighting the government.[75] The aim was to expose the ill effects of apartheid and to garner all the support from both the African continent and the globe. Church ministers in addition to the support they offered to the struggle stalwarts and organisations in South Africa, they also provided various other support such as spiritually, emotionally and financially and in some instances the church ministers had to play the role of fathers and mothers. This was by adopting the families of comrades who went into exile.[76] Furthermore, the church ministers also travelled abroad to lobby support from the international community to impose sanctions on the South African government, in order for the apartheid government to stop with the oppression of black people in South Africa. To mention just a few in this regard it will include the well-respected

70. S. Ndlovu, *The Soweto Uprising: The Road to Democracy in South Africa*, 3 South African Democratic Trust 344 (2011).
71. Kauuova, *supra* n. 70, at 4.
72. *Ibid.*
73. *South African History Online Place of Birth of Nelson Mandela*, www.sahistory.org.za (accessed 5 Jun. 2018).
74. *Ibid.*
75. Coertzen, *supra* n. 68, at 128.
76. *Ibid.*, at 129.

noble peace prize laureate Archbishop Desmond Tutu and Rev. Frank Chikana.[77] They are not the only ones. Many ministers and other church formations established by missionaries played a central role in the liberation of South Africa. Church leaders and ministers were also not spared from the apartheid brutality as some were torched, arrested, harassed, assaulted, and at some point, some of the churches were destroyed.[78] This was attributed to the fact that now churches were seen as a threat by the apartheid government and churches who opposed apartheid had to be eliminated. Religion was used as a vehicle for the emancipation of the black community from the start of the revolution until the end of this period. This was because at some point when most struggle stalwarts like Nelson Mandela, Govan Mbeki and Walter Sisulu were arrested religious leaders were working with the ANC and other liberation movements underground to keep the emancipation of black people a reality because it was in danger of being extinct through their imprisonment.[79] During the imprisonment of various political leaders, religious leaders played a role in ensuring that the struggle did not end. This was through securing funding for political parties, paying visits to political prisoners and going to hospitals to visit the injured in order to keep the struggle alive and relevant at that particular time. Furthermore, religious leaders were actively involved in conducting mass funerals caused by the apartheid government which was instrumental in killing of black people in big numbers, and an example to note is the 16 June 1976 Soweto uprising which cost the lives of thousands of young people.[80]

31. Religious leaders at the dark time of South Africa brought the necessary light using religion in order to keep the country sane and alive. Prayer sessions were held across the length and breadth of South Africa, for the almighty God to intercede on behalf of the African people who were in desperate need of liberation and freedom from their oppressors. This history and role of religion in the social makeup of the South African community can best be described as a period similar to that of the children of Israel who were slaves in Egypt. Moses, who was their Shepherd as anointed by God, managed to take them out of slavery because they were the children or a nation that was favoured by God.[81] The prayer, which religious leaders and the struggle stalwarts engaged in, was that if God can deliver the children of Israel surely He could liberate the people of South Africa from the hands of their oppressors in their country of birth. It is important to bear in mind that it will not be correct to say that the only source for the liberation of South Africa emanates from religion. Other factors and role players were also instrumental in the liberation movement. However, the point is that religion played a significant role when it comes to the emancipation of black people from the hands of the oppressors. Even though religion, which came through other means, was or is considered foreign in the African continent,, it can be said that it is one of those things or aspects that

77. *Archbishop Desmond Tutu Is Awarded the Nobel Peace Prize*, https://www.sahistory.org.za/dated-event/archbishop-desmond-tutu-awarded-nobel-peace-prize (accessed 13 Sep. 2018).
78. Coertzen, *supra* n. 68, at 130.
79. Kauuova, *supra* n. 70, at 5.
80. Ndlovu, *supra* n. 71, at 344.
81. Chapter 3 *Exodus* Verses 11–15. God hears the cries of his children and delivers them from the hands of their oppressor.

played a significant role in the freedom of South Africa. The pluralistic nature of the South African community did not hinder the role religious practices played in the liberation of South Africa. This is because the Muslim religious community and Hindu religious community joined in the struggle with the aim of ensuring that apartheid is defeated. Members from the Muslim and Hindu communities also joined the various struggle organisations like the ANC with the aim of liberating South Africa.[82] These collective efforts from different religious background affirm that religion as a practice is about collective effort and attaining social cohesion through peaceful process irrespective of where one comes from.

32. The religion of the African people or the indigenous people of South Africa is their customary practices and culture. They worship ancestors and God, in the sense that it is believed that one cannot worship God without first having considered the ancestors. Indigenous people hold the view that the ancestors are the connector between people on earth and God.[83] The indigenous cultural practice or way of life was sidelined by the colonisers and mostly seen as barbaric and the coloniser's way of life and law, which is the common law, was imposed at the exclusion of African customary law and culture.[84] More about the African customary law or practices will be discussed extensively later on in this research work. The various tribes in South Africa include the Ndebele community, Sepedi community, Tswana community, Nguni community, North and South Sotho community, Venda community and Tsonga community. All these above-mentioned tribes or communities make the South African community and have their traditional leaders.[85] These tribes or communities are spread out across the country in the nine provinces and their leaders working with the various church leaders and political leaders were instrumental to the emancipation of South Africa. Traditional leaders, making use of traditional healers as religious and cultural practitioners of indigenous systems at some point, challenged the colonisers and won the battle. For example, the fight between the Zulu tribe and the English in Natal in which the Zulu tribe won the battle to keep their land against the land invaders at the time who were from an English background.[86] Furthermore, this affirms that African religion and culture also have a rich history when it comes to the social make-up of South Africa, and it can be said that it was also one of the driving forces in the liberation of South Africa.

33. It is important to note that most if not all of the struggle stalwarts were part of these indigenous communities that make South Africa, and making use of African religion was and is still a way of life in South Africa. Traditional leaders were also instrumental in rallying their people in the indigenous communities, largely rural areas of South Africa, to join and fight the apartheid system. This affirms that

---

82. Ndlovu, *supra* n. 71, at 345.
83. N. Mndende, *An Introduction to African Religion*, 28 Surrender 1 (2012).
84. *Ibid.*, at 2.
85. J. Kiernan, *African Traditional Religions in South Africa*, 15 De Jure 27 (2008).
86. E. Frances, *History of the Zulu War and Its Origins* 12 (Chapman and Hall 1880).

the struggle against apartheid using religion was a joint venture with the aim of liberating the people of South Africa.[87] Traditional leaders and traditional healers who are the spiritual diviners in the African communities formed alliances with church leaders and ministers from the different religious dominations with the purpose of bringing down the apartheid monster of oppression and discrimination.[88] This allegiance is continuing to this very day in the democratic dispensation with the aim of ensuring that the pluralistic nature of the South African society is not undermined, and this body is currently known as the South African Council of Churches. This body consists, or is made up, of different religious leaders in South Africa, who champion the aspect that religious dominations can be diverse in nature, but they have a common element or aspect, which is to establish peace and stability in society, irrespective of the background an individual comes from.[89] The use of religion and other measures finally brought the apartheid regime to its knees and it was an end to this cruel system in 1994, which is the period known as the new dawn and the democratic dispensation of South Africa. From the above assessments, it is very much clear that religion, which is the focus of this book, is central to the liberation of South Africa, without under estimating the importance of other role players like the various political parties, international community and investors. They all played a significant role but religion managed to bring people from diverse background together to fight the common enemy, which was the terrible apartheid system. Focus will now shift to the post-apartheid period and still outlining the relevance and importance of religion in the new dawn, which is the democratic dispensation of South Africa post-1994.

B. Post-Apartheid Period

34. After the defeat of apartheid in South Africa using religion among other things, this was now the time for liberation and freedom. South Africa is now under the rule and control of the Constitution, which is the supreme law of the land.[90] Religion still has relevance and it plays an important role during this period. This is because the struggle against apartheid was fought through religion and won through the practice of religion among other things, which meant that religion remained in the centre stage of everything. Religion by its very nature champions for reconciliation and forgiveness, and in South Africa this was no different. The Truth and Reconciliation Commission (TRC) was formed and chaired by Archbishop Desmond Tutu with the aim of ensuring that the oppressor asks for forgiveness to the victims with the aim of reconciling both black and white people.[91] The purpose was to ensure that both black and white people are given the opportunity to talk about the

87. *Ibid.*
88. *Ibid.*, at 13.
89. Mndende, *supra* n. 84, at 3.
90. Section 2 of the Constitution.
91. S. Peter, *Restorative Justice and the South African Truth and Reconciliation Commission*, 32 SA Journal of Philosophy 35 (2006).

painful past they suffered and reconcile them in order to build a new South Africa through the mechanism of forgiveness, which is embedded in religion.[92]

The establishment of the TRC at the dawn of democracy affirms the important role religion has in the history and social aspect of South Africa. Hence one cannot discuss religion from a social aspect while excluding the historical aspect because they both share identical aspects and cannot be separated but can be viewed as hand in glove. Today in South Africa when one looks or assesses the position of religion it can best be described as firmly protected and enshrined in the Constitution and through various statutory provisions. For example, section 15 of the Constitution states that everyone has a right to choose their religion or belief freely.[93] The independence of the individual and religion is protected by the Constitution, and this constitutional provision and other provisions that have been set by the government of the day to ensure the independence of religion will be explored in depth later in the following chapters. However, it is important to note that religious organisations like churches enjoy autonomy and are tax exempted in South Africa as they are considered non-profit organisations who aim to bring the necessary social cohesion for all the people of South Africa.[94]

35. From the diverse religious communities, which South Africa comprises of, and as they are part of the population of South Africa for statistical purposes, it is important to consider the following aspects. The Christian community is the majority in South Africa and consists mostly of people from the indigenous communities, and are largely black people. This does not mean that only black people are Christians because white people are also Christians and this does not mean that all white and black people are Christians. There are exceptions to the general rule or norm while bearing in mind that freedom of religion is guaranteed in South Arica.[95] The Christian community is followed by the Muslim and Hindu religions respectively, who are a minority.[96] The fact that the Christian religion is the one that is dominating in South Africa does not mean that minority religious groups or organisations must be discriminated against or oppressed because religious freedom and practice is not based on numbers but it is based on the fundamental right that is guaranteed by the Constitution. Religious practices and way of life still dominate how people relate in South Africa. Religious and cultural practices are starting to be introduced in schools around South Africa, and this initiative is laying a solid foundation for the development and sustainability of religion and cultural practices in South Africa.

92. The TRC was based on the foundation of restorative justice and it is argued that this process in some cases it was not effective because there are still lots of social ills in South Africa, which includes for example racism. *See* Peter, *supra* n. 92 at 36.
93. Section 15 of the Constitution.
94. Section 21 of the Companies Act 68 of 2008.
95. Section 15 of the Constitution.
96. Coertzen, *supra* n. 68, at 130.

III. Conclusion

36. Religious and cultural practices form a part of the hybrid community of South Africa and have been used successfully in bringing the necessary stability and social cohesion that is key to the development of South Africa. Religious and cultural practices have proven to be the connector of different people with different backgrounds to share a common goal, which in the South African context was to defeat the apartheid government. Furthermore, in the new democratic dispensation religion is one of the fundamental rights that is protected by the Constitution and must be respect at all costs owing to its historical roots to the development and history of South Africa. The same can be said about cultural practices in the new constitutional dispensation. In the next chapter, reference will be made to the Constitutional position and recognition of religious practices in South Africa from a legal point of view.

Part I. Legal Framework and Sources

Chapter 1. Constitutional Position of Religion

§1. Introduction

37. Religion and religious practices form a part of the democratic dispensation of South Africa, due to the role religion played in the liberation movement of the country. Today, in the democratic dispensation religious practices are one of the fundamental rights that are protected and enshrined in the Constitution and other pieces of legislation. This without a doubt affirms the importance and independence of religious practices in the new constitutional order. Religion is a way of life or a lifestyle that is embedded in how people relate with each other from the same religious group and beyond in order to reach or connect with other people from other religious affiliations. This important aspect of religious practices being a neutraliser and a connector of different people from different lifestyles is what is championed in the South African jurisdiction through the affirmation or guarantee that is afforded to everyone when it comes to the right or freedom to choose any religion of one's choice without being forced or pushed to do so.[97]

38. Freedom of religion as a point of departure is important to note that it is guaranteed by the Constitution, which is the supreme law of the land. This means that any religion or religious practice found to be contrary to the Constitution will be declared invalid.[98] In this chapter focus will be placed on the position of religious and cultural practices from a constitutional point of view, and this will entail discussing in detail the various constitutional provisions that are aimed at the protection and promotion of religion in South Africa. Various court cases will also be discussed where the right to religion from both a legal and a social perspective are considered.

§2. The Right to Religion and Culture

39. Before getting into the discussion in connection with the constitutional protection of the right to religion and religious practices, it is important to first define what religion is as a starting point. This will enable one to have a comprehensive

97. Section 15 of the Constitution.
98. Section 2 of the Constitution.

understanding of this diverse and yet important concept called religion. It is important to note and acknowledge that religion is not defined in the Constitution, and there is no generally accepted definition that is provided either by the international law or by instruments when it comes to this definition.[99] Religion can be defined as diverse ways of being human and there are many various ways of being religious.[100] All religions are concerned with ways of seeing and being in the world and it is clear from this definition that the value of religion lies with people who are following that religion to observe the various facets that are connected with that particular religion. Three facets can be identified which are connected with religion: first, religion as a belief comes from the aspect of the existence of a deity or the adherence to doctrines and this rests with in most cases of African cultural practices or religion.[101] Second, religion is considered as a way of life and this facet puts emphasis on actions and practices that distinguish the believer from other religious dominations. In this case, for example, a Christian is prohibited to engage in adultery or polygamy as prohibited by the Bible, but this conduct is allowed in cases where a the believer is a member of the African cultural practices or belief.[102] The third and last facet is based on the aspect that religion is an identity, which focuses on the self-worth of an individual who forms part of the religious or cultural group. This means that an individual believer remains an individual despite being a member of a religious or cultural group, and this does not entail that the individual is now non-existent when it comes to the group.[103] Individual identity and freedom is protected by the Constitution as it will be outlined below when the constitutional provisions in connection to religion are discussed.

40. Section 15 of the Constitution states that everyone has a right to choose their own religion.[104] This means that each and every citizen in the Republic will be able to choose his or her religion without being put under pressure, but this also means that to partake in a religious practice is a voluntary process which an individual must exercise. The right to choose one's religious practices in South Africa goes hand in hand with other fundamental rights which are enshrined and protected by the Constitution. All the rights outlined in the Constitution do not operate in isolation but complement each other to a lesser and greater extent. This also applies to the right to choose one's own religion freely without any undue influence and this is affirmed by section 16 of the Constitution. Section 16 of the Constitution states that everyone has a right to freedom of religion and expression.[105] This provision emphasises the above-mentioned point that rights in the Constitution work hand in hand with the aim of enhancing and protecting the interests of members of the community.

---

99. I. Chipkin & A. Leatt, *Religion and Revival in Post-apartheid South Africa*, 9 RESA 39 (2009).
100. *Ibid.*
101. Mndende, *supra* n. 84, at 3.
102. All customary marriages are polygamous in nature and one husband is permitted to get married to more than one wife at a particular time. *See* Mndende, *supra* n. 84, at 4.
103. Chipkin & Leatt, *supra* n. 100, at 39.
104. Section 15 of the Constitution.
105. Section 16 of the Constitution.

41. This is attributed to the fact that section 15 gives the right to an individual the right to choose his or her own religion and religious practices, and section 16 of the Constitution strengthens this choice which the individual enjoys in connection with choosing their religion and religious practices. By focusing on the freedom and voluntariness of an individual in choosing his or her religious practices without any undue influence, it can be argued or seen as a way of affirming the autonomy of the individual person when it comes to their freedom to religion. The right to choose one's own religion and freedom in relation to that religion was tested in various court cases in South Africa, but only the landmark court cases will be considered. In *Christian Lawyers Association v. Minister of Health*,[106] the facts were in connection with the legality of abortion in South Africa. The argument that was advanced by the Christian Lawyers Association was that abortion is morally wrong and constitutes a violation of the right to life as protected by the Constitution.[107] In response, the government argued that abortion was not contrary to the right to life on the basis that a foetus does not qualify as a human being. Furthermore, abortion was a personal and voluntary choice on the part of an individual. The court held that the Choice on Termination of Pregnancy Act was indeed lawful and did not contravene any provisions as alleged and this application was dismissed by the court.[108]

42. However, in *Hay v. B*,[109] the parents of the child who was in desperate need of a blood transfusion to save his life refused the medical procedure on religious basis.[110] The parents of the child refused the blood transfusion on religious grounds as they were members of Jehovah witness church which prohibits blood transfusions.[111] Since the medical practitioner could not get the consent of the parents, there was nothing that he or she could do to save the life of the child, and if the medical practitioner acted contrary to this it would be seen as a violation of the right to religious practices according to section 15 of the Constitution, which was the basis of the arguments that were raised by the parents of the minor child.[112]

This court case took place while the legal system of South Africa was still developing and in the infancy stages. In the years that followed, there was a development in the law in terms of legislation. For example, the introduction of the Children's Act 38 of 2005, which focuses on the best interests of children irrespective of their background, religion and socio-economic circumstances.[113] The adoption of the Children's Act and the application of section 28 of the Constitution, which deals with the best interests of all children, changed the position of children and their parents especially when it comes to life-threatening situations. This meant that parents could not refuse medical treatment for their children anymore on religious grounds.

106. *Christian Lawyers Association v. Minister of Health* 1998 (11) BCLR 1434 (T), 1998 (4) SA 1113 (T).
107. *Ibid.*
108. *Christian Lawyers Association Case, supra* n. 107, at 1114.
109. *Hay v. B* 2003 (3) SA 492 (W).
110. *Ibid.*, 1114.
111. *Ibid.*
112. *Hay Case, supra* n. 110, at 1115.
113. Section 2 of the Children's Act 38 of 2005.

The medical practitioner can approach the court for permission to administer treatment to that child, because the right to life supersede the right to religion on the basis of public policy. This happened in 2014 when the Centre for Child Law at the University of Pretoria was requested by a medical practitioner to help him approach the court in order to save the life of a child who was in desperate need of blood transfusion and the court granted this order on the basis of section 28 of the Constitution.[114] From these court cases it is very much clear that a balancing exercise is key in connection to the various constitutional rights.

43. It is important to note that in South Africa one cannot discuss the position of religious practices without making reference to cultural practices. This is because as indicated earlier both religion and culture are linked to the belief systems of people who subscribe to either religion or culture in the African sense. Section 30 of the Constitution states that everyone has a right to choose the cultural group or practice of his or her own.[115] Furthermore, this constitutional provision on the right to culture is strengthened by section 31 of the Constitution, which affirms the freedom of everyone when it comes to taking part in a cultural practice or group.[116] Religion and culture are one and the same thing and this is affirmed by the definition of culture. Culture is defined as a way of life that is common to a group of people, a collection of beliefs and attitudes, shared understandings and a pattern of behaviour that allow people to live together in peace but set them apart from other people.[117] It is very much clear that both religion and culture are one because they both have to do with a lifestyle and subscribing to the cultural and religious pattern of a certain group.

44. Owing to the painful history of South Africa as already discussed above, culture and cultural practices are associated with black Africans and governed by African customary law. For a culture or cultural practice to be recognised in South Africa, it must fulfil the following requirements: The custom must have existed for a long time; the community at large must recognise the custom; the custom must be reasonable; and the custom must be consistent and subject to the Constitution and other legislation.[118] These standards as set out by the legislature aim to ensure that culture is not abused, and in particular African customary law because it is largely unwritten. These conditions do not aim to undermine the right to culture of indigenous people but aim to safeguard this right from abuse. Cultural practices could be in most instances associated with indigenous people, but sections 30 and 31 respectively of the Constitution by stating everyone it means that people from different backgrounds and ethnic groups are free to partake in cultural practices of indigenous people.[119] This is because to take part in either culture or religion is a voluntary process and it only lies with the individual. Even though these standards as set out by the Constitution in connection with the recognition of culture are not

114. Section 28 of the Constitution.
115. Section 30 of the Constitution.
116. Section 31 of the Constitution.
117. Mndende, *supra* n. 84, at 6.
118. *Ibid.*, at 7.
119. Section 30 of the Constitution and s. 31 of the Constitution.

explicitly outlined for religion, it can be argued that for a religious group to be protected by the Constitution it is necessary that it meet the standards as outlined above. More about the position of African customary law, which gives rise to culture, will be explored later. The right to choose culture and the freedom that is associated with choosing such a culture are not absolute and this is also the case when it comes to religion and can be limited by section 36 of the Constitution as the general limitation clause.[120]

45. Apart from the rights and freedom to choose religion and culture, other fundamental rights are key as already outlined in realising and protecting religion or cultural practices. Focus will now shift to those fundamental rights with the aim of protecting as well as promoting the rights to religion and cultural practices from a South African point of view.

§3. The Right to Dignity and Equality in Realisation of the Right to Religion and Culture

46. Section 10 of the Constitution states that everyone has inherent dignity and the right to have their dignity respected and protected.[121] Further, it is important to enquire what human dignity means. It is defined as an individual's or a group's feeling, its self-respect and self-worth. Human dignity is concerned with physical and psychological integrity and empowerment, and is harmed or violated by unfair treatment premised upon personal traits or circumstances, which do not relate to individual needs, capacities or merits. The right to human dignity is enhanced by laws, which are sensitive to the needs, capacities and merits of different individuals, taking into account the context of their differences.[122] The right to human dignity is harmed or violated when people are marginalised, ignored or devalued, and it is enhanced when laws recognise the full place of all individuals and groups within society. Religious and cultural practices are protected because they are central to human dignity.[123] Scholars like Lenaghan argue that due to the racial discrimination past of South Africa it is important that human dignity should be highly valued as a constant reminder of the past inequality and discrimination.[124] This is due to the impact of the past inequality and discrimination on the values of indigenous cultural and religious practices. Furthermore, it is important to consider what does equality in the context of religion and cultural practices really entail before linking both the right to human dignity and equality in realising the right to culture and religion.

120. Section 36 of the Constitution is the general limitation clause and it will be discussed extensively later on.
121. Section 10 of the Constitution.
122. T. Asad, *Discipline and Reasons of Power in Christianity Formations and Dignity* 34, (John Hopkins University 2006).
123. *Ibid.*, at 35.
124. C. Lenaghan, *Shots in the Streets: Violence and Religion in South Africa, Contemporary South African Debates* 68, (Oxford University Press 2004).

47. Section 9(1) of the Constitution states that everyone is equal before the law and has the right to equal protection and benefit of the law.[125] De Vos and Freedman argue that the right to equality can best be described in two ways. First, the right to equality does not entail a guarantee that all people should be treated identically all the time, regardless of their personal attributes or characteristics, social or economic status. The right should therefore be viewed as entailing more than a formal prohibition against discrimination. Second, the right to equality must guarantee more than equality before the law and must focus on the effects or impact of legal rules or other differentiating treatment on people. The right to equality cannot therefore focus merely on whether two or more people have been treated in an identical manner by the legal rule or by the company or another individual concerned.[126] One can assert that this two-stage enquiry in relation to the meaning of equality is balanced and in line with the principle of substantive equality.[127] For the purposes of this research project and of relevance when discussing the equality clause is section 9(3) of the Constitution which provides that the state may not unfairly discriminate directly or indirectly against anyone on one or more grounds, including race, gender, sexual orientation, age, religion, belief, disability, culture, language and birth.[128] From the above discussion of both the right to dignity and equality, it is important to note that the right to equality plays an important role in the recognition of dignity and both are fundamental. Accordingly, from this assertion, there is a connection between dignity and privacy and this view was confirmed in *Christian Education South Africa v. Minister of Education*.[129] In this case, it was held that equality does not require that we treat everyone equal but that we treat everyone with equal concern and respect irrespective of his or her religious or cultural practices.[130] Goldstone J, in this case, summarised the importance or connection between dignity and equality in the following way:

> At the heart of the prohibition of unfair discrimination lies a recognition that the purpose of our new constitutional and democratic order is the establishment of a society in which all the human beings will be accorded equal dignity and respect regardless of their membership in a particular group.[131]

48. This court case like many others and the constitutional provisions, which aim to champion the realisation of religious and cultural practices, can be seen as a way of remedying the past injustices while at the same time ensuring that the new democratic order upholds the fundamental rights of the people of South Africa. It is also important to consider that dignity is not only defined in different ways, but it also operates in different respects. Dignity can function as a specific right as

---

125. Section 9(1) of the Constitution.
126. P. De Vos and M. Freedman, *South African Constitutional Law* 421, (Oxford University Press, Cape Town 2015).
127. *Ibid.*, at 422.
128. Section 9(3) of the Constitution.
129. *Christian Education South Africa v. Minister of Education* [2000] ZACC 11, 2000 (4) SA 757 (CC); 2000 (10) BCLR 1051 (CC).
130. *Ibid.*
131. *Ibid.*, at 1052.

entrenched in section 10 of the Constitution.[132] Additionally, dignity may determine how the entrenched right like the right to choose religion and cultural practices without any form of discrimination in order to achieve equality can be practiced.[133] This means that dignity can serve as a basis to the realisation of a fundamental right that is upheld and protected by the Constitution, which in this case is the right to choose cultural and religious practices of one's choice. This is often the reason in South Africa that dignity is classified as a value because different provisions in the Bill of Rights must be interpreted in order to promote the values that underlie a democratic society. These values include human dignity, equality and freedom.[134] Without a doubt, it is clear that human dignity lies in the heart of the new democratic order of South Africa.

49. Dignity therefore stands in relation to the application of all other rights and these rights shape our understanding of dignity. For this reason, dignity has particular relevance to our understanding of the right to freedom of religion and culture. Similarly, the right to equality is of particular importance to our appreciation of the right to freedom of religion and culture as outlined. The interrelationship between dignity and equality in many ways can be comparable to the interrelation that exists between religion and culture as explored. For diversity to prosper it is essential that the value of dignity and equality as well as the interrelation between religion and culture are held when addressing issues regarding the manifestation of indigenous culture and religion, in particular.

§4. The Right to Privacy and Right to Religion and Cultural Practices

50. Before discussing the right to privacy in South African law, it is important to consider that the Constitution entrenches this right in section 14.[135] Furthermore, it is necessary to take into consideration that the right to privacy is also upheld and protected by various statutes, including the Protection of Personal Information Act and the National Health Act.[136] More about the role of these two statutes will be explored later when discussing the position of domestic legislations that are in place in relation with the protection of religion and cultural practices.

132. Section 10 of the Constitution.
133. Section 15 of the Constitution.
134. Section 2 of the Constitution.
135. Section 14 of the Constitution and s. 2(a) of the Protection of Personal Information Act 4 of 2013 (herewith referred to as Poppy) set out the purpose of this Act by outlining that the aim of this Act is to give effect to the constitutional right to privacy, by safeguarding personal information when processed by a responsible party, subject to justifiable limitations that are aimed at balancing the right to privacy against other rights, particularly the right of access to information and protecting important interests, including free flow of information within the Republic and across international borders.
136. Section 2 of Poppy and s. 14 of the National Health Act 61 of 2003.

I. Common Law Definition of Privacy

51. Under common law, every person has personality rights such as the rights to physical integrity, freedom, reputation, dignity and privacy.[137] According to Neethling, privacy is defined as an individual condition of a person's life, which is characterised by seclusion from the public and publicity.[138] Since privacy is considered as personal facts which a person has determined to exclude from the knowledge of other people, this means that the right to privacy can only be violated when a person learns of the true private facts of another person against his or her will.[139]

52. The right to privacy has long been entrenched in the common law, in which everyone has personality rights which include the right to physical integrity, freedom, reputation, dignity and privacy.[140] This right to privacy has been recognised as an independent personal right that applies to both natural persons and juristic persons, such as companies.[141] The violation of the right to privacy is determined by the court, in terms of the reasonable standard in the interests of the community in order to guard against any form of injustices on an individual or a company.[142] Privacy underpins dignity since a violation of the right to privacy infringes on the right to dignity.[143] This is because these two rights relate to each other, in the sense that the right to privacy ensures that one maintains confidential information that he or she has, and if such information is published in a derogatory manner it will damage the dignity of the person.[144]

53. This rich history, which emanates from common law with regard to the right to privacy and other related rights such as dignity and reputation, clearly affirms Burchell's view that 'the common law of privacy in South Africa still provide the lion's share when it comes to the right to privacy standard'.[145] This is despite the fact that currently in the new constitutional dispensation, the rights to privacy, dignity, reputation and freedom are recognised individually and independently in order to give them more recognition and further interpretation; this was not the position in common law previously as these rights were treated collectively rather than individually.[146]

---

137. J. Neethling, J.M. Potgieter & P.J. Visser, *Neethling's Law of Personality* 31 (Butterworths, Durban 2005).
138. *Ibid.*, at 32.
139. A. Roos, *Personal Data Protection in New Zealand: Lessons for South Africa*, 4 PER/PELJ 191 (2008).
140. *Ibid.*, at 192.
141. Neethling et al., *supra* n. 138, at 37.
142. *Ibid.*, at 38.
143. Section 10 of the Constitution.
144. *C v. Minister of Correctional Services* 1996 (4) SA 292 (T).
145. J.M. Burchell, *Media Freedom of Expression Scores as Strict Liability Receives the Red Card: National Media Ltd v. Bogoshi*, 8 SALJ 1 (1999).
146. Section 14 of the Constitution and s. 12 of the Constitution it protects everyone's right to freedom and security.

II. Legality of the Common Law Right to Privacy in the Constitutional Era

54. Section 8(3) of the Constitution provides that when applying a provision of the Bill of Rights to either a natural or juristic person, a court must apply, or if necessary, develop the common law to the extent that legislation does not give effect to the right under consideration, in order to properly give effect thereto.[147] Furthermore, a court may develop the rules of common law to limit a right, provided the limitation is in line with section 36(1) of the Constitution. Section 39(3) of the Constitution, which deals with the interpretation of the Bill of Rights,[148] states that the Bill of Rights does not deny the existence of any other rights or freedoms that are recognised or conferred by the common law, customary law or legislation to the extent that they are consistent with the Bill of Rights. These constitutional provisions clearly affirm the view that Burchell holds about the common law carrying a lion's share on the right to privacy, as outlined.

55. However, the common law position with regard to the right to privacy still needs the affirmation of the Constitution before it might be used as a point of departure. The common law right to privacy can be limited as well as declared null and void if it is found to be contrary to the provisions of the Constitution.[149] The position is quite clear that although the common law right to privacy in South Africa is fundamental due to its historical scope, it is however subject to the Constitution which is the crucial aspect that Burchell omitted in his assessment of the position of common law right to privacy.

56. The right to privacy has long been protected in our law dating back to the time it was inherited from the Roman law system in which the *actio iniuriarum* was provided as a remedy in cases where there was an invasion to the sanctity of a person's home.[150] This has been the position before the constitutional dispensation came into existence and provided for the right to privacy in section 14 of the Constitution.[151] Two examples of case decisions dealing with the common law right to privacy can be found in the 1900s. First, an English case will be discussed and then a South African decision thereafter.

Tolly v. Fry and Sons Ltd [1931] AC 333

147. Section 8(3) read with s. 8(2) of the Constitution.
148. Section 39(3) of the Constitution.
149. Section 2 of the Constitution.
150. Neethling et al., *supra* n. 138, at 38. The remedy with regard to the *actio iniuriarum*, which owes its historical development to Roman law, was established and used to recover damages (*solatium*) based on the intentional infringements of one of the acknowledged personality rights. In order to succeed with this remedy, an infringement of a legally acknowledged interest of personality is required and such infringement has to be intentional in the process. *See Jackson v. NICRO* 1976 3 SA 1 (A) 11, in which the history and purpose of this Roman remedy was clearly outlined and applied with the aim of making an informed decision in the process.
151. Section 14 of the Constitution.

57. In *Tolly v. Fry and Sons Ltd,*[152] the plaintiff was an amateur golfer and the defendant was a producer of candy. The defendant, in his advertisement of chocolates, showed the plaintiff with a protruding bar of chocolate in his back pocket.[153] This form of advertisement was not done with the consent of the plaintiff and the plaintiff challenged this on the basis that it violated his right to dignity and privacy. Furthermore, the plaintiff argued that such advertisement was done without his consent, and that it had the potential to destroy his golfing career as he was still an amateur, due to the misleading nature of the advertisement.[154] The court found the conduct of the defendant as unlawful and ordered the defendant to compensate the plaintiff for the loss or harm which he had suffered as a result of the advertisement.[155]

***O'Keeffe v. Argus Printing and Publishing Company Ltd* 1954 (3) SA 244 (C)**

58. In *O'Keeffe v. Argus Printing and Publishing Company Ltd,*[156] the plaintiff was a well-known radio personality who consented to the publication of her photograph, taken at the pistol range, to be used for a newspaper article by the defendant company.[157] The defendant company, however, used the photograph of the plaintiff for advertising purposes, which was not what the plaintiff consented to in the first place. Watermeyer AJ held the view that the conduct of the respondent company was unlawful and that the respondent acted contrary to the right to privacy of the plaintiff and was ordered to compensate the plaintiff for the violation of her right to privacy with regard to the derogatory advertisement.[158]

III. The Right to Privacy in Section 14 of the Constitution of the Republic of South Africa, 1996

59. Section 14 of the Constitution states that everyone has the right to privacy, which includes the right not to have their person or their home searched; their property searched; their possession seized; or the privacy of their communications infringed.[159] This provision of the Constitution, which guarantees the right to privacy, is supported by Schoeman who defines privacy as a state or condition of limited access to a person.[160] Furthermore, the right to privacy was explained in *National Media Ltd ao v. Jooste.*[161] Harms AJ explained that the right to privacy

152. *Tolly v. Fry and Sons Ltd* [1931] AC 333; [1931] UKHL 1.
153. *Tolly Case, supra* n. 153, at 334.
154. *Ibid.*
155. *Tolly Case, supra* n. 153, at 335.
156. *O'Keeffe v. Argus Printing and Publishing Company Ltd* 1954 (3) SA 244 (C).
157. *Ibid.*
158. *Ibid.*, at 245.
159. Section 14 of the Constitution.
160. F. Schoeman, *Philosophical Dimensions of Privacy: An Anthology* 5 (Cambridge University Press, Cambridge 1984).
161. *National Media Ltd ao v. Jooste* 1996 (3) SA 262 (A).

can best be described as an individual condition of life characterised from the public and publicity. This condition includes all personal facts which the individual has determined to exclude from the knowledge of other people and in respect of which he or she has wills that they be kept private.[162] *Kennedy and Arnold v. Ireland*[163] takes the discussion of the right to privacy further by stating that:

> ... though not specifically guaranteed by the Constitution, the right to privacy is one of the fundamental personal rights of the citizen which flow from the Christian and democratic nature of the state. The nature of the right to privacy must be such as to ensure the dignity and freedom of an individual in the type of society envisaged by the Constitution, namely a sovereign, independent and democratic society.[164]

60. This reasoning by the court surely envisages the position of the South African jurisprudence, in protecting the right to privacy of an individual from other people in a democratic state. Furthermore, this means the right to privacy of an individual as a member of a religious group is protected and this extends to the religious organisation.

IV. The Limitation of Constitutional Rights

A. Rationale for the Limitation of Rights

61. In a democratic state where the Constitution is the supreme law of the country, it is important that there must be a balance between the rights and duties which citizens enjoy for democracy to function.[165] This will entail limiting the rights of other people in the public's interest through a general limitation clause. Rautenbach and Malherbe argue that there can be no peace and order in any society when people's rights are exercised absolutely without limitations.[166] However, it is important to take into account that the limitation of rights must not be arbitrary, but needs to be in line with the Constitution, taking into account values such as human dignity, equality and freedom.[167] Devenish explains the background of the general limitation clause, and particularly, what it entails and its purpose.[168] He outlines that:

> It is widely accepted in the domestic law of most countries, in international law and according to international and other human rights documents, that only a very limited number of rights, if any [,] are absolute. These include freedom from torture, the abuse and exploitation of children and possibly freedom from

162. *Ibid.*, at 263.
163. *Kennedy and Arnold v. Ireland* [1987] IR 587.
164. *Ibid.*
165. Section 2 of the Constitution.
166. C. Rautenbach & R. Malherbe, *Constitutional Law* 156 (LexisNexis, Cape Town 2015).
167. Section 36(1) of the Constitution.
168. G.E. Devenish, *A Commentary on the South African Constitution* 121 (Butterworths, Durban 1998).

servitude; freedom of conscience, belief, thought and opinion. The overwhelming majority of human rights and liberties which are of necessity are restricted by inherent duty, which should be perceived as the inextricable counterpart of a corresponding right, to respect the rights of others. The classical example in this instance is that freedom of speech does not allow one person to defame another nor would it [call for a] sanction [to be imposed on] a person shouting fire in a full theatre when there is no fire.[169]

62. This means that there must be a link between a right and the means by which it is limited in order for it to be considered a lawful and justifiable limitation.

In addition, section 38 of the Constitution provides that anyone whose rights have been infringed can seek appropriate relief from a court or tribunal. Sections 36(1) and 38 of the Constitution set out the tone for dealing with the issue of the limitation clause, which is applicable in the relationships between the state and private individuals, as well as in the relationships between private individuals themselves. The next step will be to look into the limitation clause and also to make an enquiry as to whether it is valid or not.

B. The General Limitation Clause in Section 36(1) of the Constitution of the Republic of South Africa, 1996

63. Section 8 of the Constitution is important in describing the relationship between the state and private individuals.[170] This section facilitates a more realistic way of dealing with the rights of all people and balancing them with the obligations of the state. For example, section 14 of the Constitution does not grant people an absolute right as the state can violate the right to privacy of the individual with the aim of protecting the public's interests.

64. Similar to any other rights contained in the Constitution, the right to privacy can be limited according to section 36(1) thereof. This section provides the general limitation clause and states that the rights in the Bill of Rights may be limited only in terms of the law of general application to the extent that the limitation is reasonable and justifiable in an open and democratic society based on human dignity, equality and freedom. This limitation ought to be effected while taking into account factors such as the nature of the right. This means the purpose of the right; the importance of the purpose of the limitation, which has to do with the reason behind limiting the right; the nature and extent of the limitation, which has to do with an enquiry (which is normally done by the court) into looking at the way the limitation

169. *Ibid*
170. Section 8(1) of the Constitution states that the Bill of Rights applies to all laws. The Bill of Rights binds all the branches and spheres of government bodies. This means that it must be followed by: (a) the legislatures, which is a body that makes law; (b) the executive, which is the body that carries out law; (c) the judiciary, which are the courts. Section 8(2) of the Constitution states that the Bill of Rights applies to all matters between citizens and the government. This means it applies vertically between citizens and the government. The Bill of Rights also applies horizontally in matters which arise among people or businesses.

took place; the relation between the limitation and its purpose, meaning that there must be a balance between the infringement of a right and its purpose in order for the limitation to be justifiable; and the less restrictive means to achieve the purpose, which means that the limitation must achieve benefits which are proportional to the impact of that limitation.[171]

65. However, it is important to note that in *National Coalition for Gay and Lesbian Equality and Another v. Minister of Justice and Others*,[172] the court held that the limitation of gay rights on moral grounds was not proportional to the benefits that were aimed to be achieved. In this case the court held that, the enforcement of private moral views of a section of the community, which is based to a large extent on prejudice, cannot qualify to be a legitimate purpose.[173] There is nothing, in the proportionality enquiry, to weigh against the extent of the limitation and its harmful impact on gays. In this case the court stated that there is no justification for the limitation of gay rights.[174]

66. The operation of section 36 of the Constitution can be illustrated using the example of a medical practitioner who discloses the health status of a patient who has acquired the Ebola virus to other people. In this instance, the disclosure can be justified as acting in the public interest in order to curb the spread of the virus. Furthermore, an equitable balance exists between the purpose of the disclosure and the limitation of the right to privacy, given the dangerous nature of the Ebola virus. Thus, such a disclosure is aimed at protecting the public's interest and ensuring that the particular patient is placed in quarantine. This will not amount to a violation of the right to privacy of the patient but can be considered a protected disclosure, according to section 36(1) of the Constitution.

67. In South African law there are court cases in which the role and legitimacy of section 36 of the Constitution have been described in detail. For example, in *S v. Manamela* the court stated that:

> In essence, the court must engage in a balancing exercise and arrive at a global judgment on proportionality and not adhere mechanically to a sequential check-list. As a general rule, the more serious the impact of the measure on the right, the more persuasive or compelling the justification must be. Unfortunately, the question is one of degree to be assessed in the concrete legislative

---

171. Section 36(1)(a)–(e) of the Constitution further argues that there is no hard and fast rule for determining whether the purpose of the limitation is considered constitutionally legitimate. However, broadly speaking the constitutional values of openness, democracy, freedom, equality and dignity will play a role in determining what a legitimate purpose is. This shows that courts will judge each case based on its own merits and decide what constitutes a legitimate purpose. Without a doubt, this is the correct approach which needs to be adopted in order to ensure that the law is in line with the public interest and that the public interest is upheld at all times.
172. *National Coalition for Gay and Lesbian Equality and Another v. Minister of Justice and Others*, (CCT11/98) [1998] ZACC 15; 1999 (1) SA 6; 1998 (12) BCLR 1517 (9 Oct. 1998).
173. *Ibid.*, at para. 37.
174. *Ibid.*, at para. 38.

and social setting of the measure, paying due regard to the means which are realistically available in our country at this stage, but without losing sight of the ultimate values to be protected. Each particular infringement of a right has different implications in an open and democratic society based on dignity, equality and freedom. There can be accordingly no absolute standard for determining reasonableness.[175]

68. However, the issue of protected disclosure in our law is a complicated matter and needs to be judged based on the facts of each case. Our courts have rejected a number of cases on the basis that the disclosure of the health status of a person is unlawful and does not amount to protected disclosure, and thus not justified in section 36 of the Constitution. For example, in *NM v. Smith*,[176] in which the Human Immunodeficiency Virus (HIV) status of three people was published in a book without their consent, the court rejected the argument raised by the respondent that the HIV status of the three applicants was known by the public, as the court held that such disclosure was not in the public's interest and thus did not amount to a protected disclosure.[177]

69. In *Maje v. Botswana Life Insurance*,[178] the plaintiff sued the defendant company for publishing her photograph in the company's newsletter and thereby depicting her as being HIV positive. The defendant company argued that it was in the public's interest to make such a disclosure, and the court dismissed such reasoning on the basis that the publication was offensive and had caused her humiliation.[179] The conduct of the defendant company did not amount to a protected disclosure and was not in the public's interest, but it amounted to an actionable offence.[180] Based on the above court cases it is clear that for a disclosure to be protected and justified, it must be in the public's interest and thus it can be argued that such a disclosure

175. *S v. Manamela and Another* 2000 (3) SA 1 (CC), 'the court stated that the limitation of constitutional rights for a purpose that is reasonable and necessary in a democratic society involves weighing up of competing values and ultimately an assessment based on proportionality. This is implicit in the provisions of S 33(1)(c) of the Interim Constitution. The fact that different rights have different implications for democracy, and in the case of our Constitution, for an open and democratic society based on freedom and equality, means that there is no absolute standard which can be laid down for determining reasonableness and necessity. Principles can be established, but the application of those principles to particular circumstances can only be done on the case-by-case basis. This is inherent in the requirement of proportionality, which calls for the balancing of different interests. In the balancing process, the relevant considerations will include the nature of the right that is limited, and its importance to an open and democratic society based on freedom and equality, the purpose for which the right is limited and the importance of that purpose to such a society, the extent of the limitation, its efficacy, and particularly where the limitation has to be necessary, whether the desired ends could reasonably be achieved through other means less damaging to the right in question. In the process, regard must be had to the provisions of section 33(1)(c) of the Interim Constitution, and the underlying values of the Constitution, bearing in mind that as a Canadian Judge has said, the role of the court is not to second-guess the wisdom of policy choices made by legislators'.
176. *NM v. Smith* Case, *supra* n. 1 at 250.
177. *Ibid.*
178. *Maje v. Botswana Life Insurance* [2001] 2 BLR 626.
179. *Ibid.*
180. *Ibid.*, at 627.

must serve a certain purpose, which is in the public's interest before it can be considered justifiable according to section 36 of the Constitution.

70. In the context of religion and culture, which are the central themes of this study, it is important to note that the rights to religion and cultural practices are not absolute for an individual or group as protected by the Constitution. This means that the right to religion and culture can be limited if it is in the public interests to do so according to section 36(1) of the Constitution.[181] The right to privacy of a religious or cultural group can be limited if it is found to be reasonable and justifiable in an open and democratic society, based on human dignity, equality and freedom. In South Africa the right to religion and religious practices was limited, for example, in the case of the Jehovah witness church on the stance of the refusal to take blood transfusion based on religious grounds. This was found to be contrary to the right to life and contrary to the public interest and hence the limitation on the right to religion as per section 15 of the Constitution.[182] It can be argued that the limitation clause is a neutraliser in keeping harmony between the rights and the limitations of rights as contained in the Constitution.

§5. Conclusion

71. The constitutional position in South Africa in relation to religion and cultural practices is without a doubt firmly entrenched and protected based on the various provisions that were explored above. This means that despite the diversity of the South African population religious and cultural practices are encouraged and promoted because religion and culture is one of those practices that are necessary and important to bring and achieve the social cohesion. It was also outlined in the chapter that despite the autonomy of an individual to choose religion and culture and freedom that come with such choice, these rights are not absolute and can be limited according to section 36 of the Constitution, which is the general limitation clause. The limitation of these rights and other fundamental rights must not be viewed as discriminatory or arbitrary to religion and culture, but the limitation itself aims to ensure that these rights are not used adversely or abused at the expense of other rights and other people, bearing in mind the pluralistic society such as South Africa.

The focus of the work will now be shifted to various legislations which are entrenched in South African law, with an aim of promoting and protecting the rights to religion and culture among other things.

181. Section 36(1) of the Constitution.
182. Section 15 of the Constitution.

Chapter 2. Legislation Aimed at the Promotion of Religion and Cultural Practices

§1. INTRODUCTION

72. The Constitution was adopted in 1996 as the supreme law of the land, which has a Bill of Rights that contains fundamental rights like the right to choose and freedom in relation to religion and culture among other things. Furthermore, in ensuring that these fundamental rights are realised section 7(3) of the Constitution mandates the government to respect, protect, promote and fulfil the rights in the Bill of Rights.[183] Religious and cultural groups also have an obligation to ensure that when they exercise their rights to choose and freedom in relation to religion and culture they comply with the conditions that have been set by the Constitution.[184]

73. After the constitutional enactment ensuring the protection of religious and cultural practices, there were questions in relation to the implications of this new position. This resulted in the formulation of the South African Charter of Religious Rights and Freedoms as one of the codes that aim to regulate religious and cultural practices from a legislative point of view. However, it is important to note that the background for the formulation of this piece of legislation emanates from Albie Sachs, a struggle stalwart who also became one of the justices in the Constitutional Court in the new dawn of democracy. Sachs wrote during the drafting period of the Constitution in 1990 in connection with the position of religious and cultural practices in South Africa:

> Ideally in South Africa, all religious organisations and persons concerned with the study of religion would get together and draft a charter of religious rights and responsibilities – it would be up to the participants themselves to define what they consider to be their fundamental rights.[185]

An in-depth discussion of this charter as to how it was formed, the purpose of the charter and how does it regulate religious and cultural practices in connection with the Constitution as the supreme law in the land will be considered.

§2. THE FORMATION OF THE SOUTH AFRICAN CHARTER OF RELIGIOUS RIGHTS AND FREEDOMS

74. This charter on Religious Rights and Freedom was drafted over a number of years, and it was a continuous process by a number of people from diverse backgrounds who make the South African community or society. This included academics, religious leaders, government commissioners, human rights groups and

183. Section 7(3) of the Constitution.
184. Section 36 of the Constitution.
185. A. Sachs, *The Soft Vengeance of a Freedom Fighter* 3 (Amazon 1990).

organisations, the international community, legal experts, media groups, and major religious and cultural groups in South Africa were consulted with.

75. After all the work was done by these various participants, then the charter was endorsed in 2010 in the presence of the then Deputy Chief Justice of South Africa, Dikgang Moseneke, who was of the view that the charter represented the diversity and religious as well as cultural freedom of the people of South Africa.[186] At the occasion, ninety-one leaders who represented different religious and cultural groups were present in order to affirm the importance of the charter when it comes to the regulation of religion and culture. Furthermore, different religious and cultural groups were present at the occasion to show solidarity to this charter which aimed to strengthen the independence and freedom of religious and cultural practices. The total number of people who were signatories for the adoption of this charter to be law in South Africa was estimated to be 10.5 million.[187] This shows that the various religious and cultural communities in South Africa welcomed the charter because it was viewed as one of those pieces of legislation that aimed to promote the independence and freedom of religious and cultural practices in South Africa. Currently, the charter is available in six of the eleven official languages of South Africa, which include English, Afrikaans, Zulu, Xhosa, Sotho and Tswana.[188] This means that work needs to be done in ensuring that the charter is written in all the eleven official languages of South Africa to ensure that it is available and accessible to all people, and language must not be a barrier when it comes to understanding and interpretation of the charter. After the public endorsement of the charter, a South African Council for the Protection and Promotion of Religious Rights and Freedoms was established to oversee the process of the charter to be formally adopted as law in South Africa.

76. The discussion about the aim and purpose of this charter, which ensures the right to choose and freedom in connection to religion and culture, will now follow.

§3. Purpose, Aim and Objective of the South African Charter of Religious Rights and Freedoms

77. The South African Charter of Religious Rights and Freedoms defines freedom, rights and responsibilities of religious and cultural beliefs and the relationship between the government of South Africa and its citizens.[189] The Bill of Rights affirms that everyone has the right to freedom of religion and culture, while section 234 of the charter makes provision for civil organisations like churches and cultural groups to draw up charters of rights and responsibilities, which may then be enacted by parliament.[190] This charter on religious rights and freedoms is the first of its kind

186. Coertzen, *supra* n. 68, at 130.
187. *Ibid.*, at 131.
188. *Ibid.*, at 132.
189. Section 1 of the South African Charter of Religious Rights and Freedom, 2010.
190. Section 234 of the South African Charter of Religious Rights and Freedom.

in South Africa and apart from addressing freedoms and rights of religion over and against the government, the charter is very useful and important for the relationship between the different religious and cultural groups in South Africa, irrespective of their diversity. The charter aims to help the different religious and cultural groups in South Africa. It is not the purpose of this charter to bring one religious belief or cultural practice in South Africa, but to strengthen diversity and independence of religious and cultural practices in South Africa.[191]

78. The charter defines the rights and freedoms that each religion or culture in the Republic can claim while at the same time working together with other religions and cultural groups in the public interest and for the common good of the entire population of South Africa, which is pluralistic in nature. The charter also serves as a useful tool in ensuring that religious and cultural groups are in a position to determine their own self-identity in terms of rights and freedoms. It is important to note that if religious and cultural groups do not make use of this tool as provided by the charter, they will find that their rights and freedoms will be determined by the courts, which can be a very difficult exercise due to the expensive nature of litigation in South Africa.[192] Even if parliament decides not to enact the charter into law, religious and cultural organisations can always make it part of their own body of rules and regulations, which then will have to be taken into account by the courts in case of a dispute.

79. The charter consists of a Preamble of eight articles, which outline the purpose of the charter. This is then followed by the charter itself, comprised of twelve articles with sub-divisions, stating the religious rights and freedoms of religious people and communities in South Africa. Furthermore, the charter states what freedom of religion means to religious believers and religious organisations in South Africa within a South African context, as well as the specific rights, responsibilities and freedoms that are associated with freedom of religion.[193] These include the following, among others:

(a) The right to gather to observe religious beliefs.
(b) Freedom of expression regarding religion.
(c) The right of citizens to change their faith.
(d) The right of persons to be educated in their faith.
(e) The right of citizens to educate their children in accordance with their philosophical and religious convictions.
(f) The right to refuse to perform certain duties or assist in activities that violate their religious belief.
(g) The rights of religions to institutional freedom.[194]

---

191. Section 1 of the South African Charter of Religious Rights and Freedom.
192. Coertzen, *supra* n. 68, at 133.
193. Section 2 of the South African Charter of Religious Rights and Freedom.
194. *Ibid.*

80. All these rights and freedoms, which are outlined in the charter, will be extensively discussed in the following chapters with the aim of showing the interrelatedness between the Constitution and the charter. This is because the aim of both these legal instruments is to ensure that the right to choose, and freedom to practice, a religion or culture is protected and promoted in the new constitutional order of South Africa.

§4. CONCLUSION

81. In conclusion, from the above assessment it is very much clear that religious and cultural practices are both constitutionally and statutorily entrenched, irrespective of the diversity of the South African society. A piece of legislation like the South African charter on religious rights and freedom aims to champion the right to freedom of religion and cultural practices in South Africa. This is while at the same time ensuring that different religious and cultural organisations work together with the purpose of protecting the freedom of religion and culture and the independence that is associated with it.

Chapter 3. Typology of the South African System

§1. Introduction

82. South Africa is a multicultural and pluralistic community with people who belong to different cultural and religious beliefs or groups. It is important to outline at this stage particularly when it has become necessary to discuss the different religious and cultural beliefs that make the South African society that all of them are equal. This means that there is no religion or cultural practice or group that dominates the other but all are equal and important before the law and the broader South African community, and this is evident from the different provisions of the Constitution that aim to strengthen and protect the independence as well as freedom of religious and cultural practices.

83. 84. In this chapter the focus will be on the classifications, outlining the different religious groups and cultural practices in South Africa in their diversity. It is important to note that emphasis will be on the African cultural practice or culture in this chapter because this forms a part of the belief of the indigenous people of South Africa. This cultural system was sidelined by the colonisers of South Africa and the effects are still felt to this very day because African customary law, which regulates the cultural practice of the indigenous people, is under-developed and not implemented to its full capacity in South Africa.

§2. Different Religious Dominations in South Africa

I. Christianity

84. Christianity is the religion of the people who follow Jesus Christ as their Saviour and Lord who together with the Father and the Holy Spirit is the True God. Out of love for the world, the Father sent the Son to the world in order to save it from sin.[195] The Son died for the sin of the world, and rose from the dead after three days of his death. As the Lord who raised from the dead, Christ is the head of the whole of creation, which is the Kingdom of God.[196] Christ was at the same time also given as the head of the church, his body, the fullness of Him that fills everything in everybody. They who believed in Him are His church and at the same time members of His Kingdom, called to witness to the world in every aspect of their life about Jesus Christ, the Lord of the whole of creation.[197] For Christians, the Bible is the Word of God which guides them in their religious and moral life in all spheres of life. It is important to note that Christianity reached South Africa very early in the Western Calendar.[198] The reformed religion came to the southern tip of

195. Holy Bible 2 Corinthians Ch 5: Verses 14–15.
196. Holy Bible Hebrews Ch 2: Verses 14.
197. R. Elphick, *Christianity in South Africa: A Political, Social and Cultural History* 11 (University of California Press 1997).
198. *Ibid.*, at 12.

Africa from Western Europe in 1652, through the establishment of a refreshment post for their ships at the Cape of Good Hope by the Dutch East Indian Company.[199] Today the majority of the population of South Africa, both black and white, follow the Christian faith as a way of life.[200]

II. Muslim

85. Muslim religion is a minority religion in the South African community as the number of people who follow the Muslim religion are estimated to be 1.5% of the total population of South Africa.[201] When tracing the historical background of the Muslim religion in the South African context, it is important to bear in mind that these were the Indians who were brought to South Africa as slaves in 1652 to work in the sugar plantations in Natal.[202] The people who subscribe to the Muslim religion are mostly in the Indian and coloured communities of South Africa, and it is important to note that they do not isolate themselves from other religious dominations; this is because inter-faith is championed.[203] Muslims use the *Qur'an* as their book of faith and believe in Mohammed as their Saviour and that of the world.[204] Even though Muslims are a minority in South Africa, their religious rights and freedoms are firmly entrenched in the Constitution. This is evident from the fact that during the recognised periods of worship like the month of Ramadan, people who form part of this religion are given the space to pray without any form of discrimination, in the workplace or schools.[205]

III. Hindu Religion

86. Hindu religion is a minority religious group in South Africa, which consists of about 1.1% of the population of South Africa.[206] Hindus arrived in South Africa during the British rule of colonisers in which they were promised good jobs and income by the then British government with the security that they will be allowed to practice their religion without disturbance.[207] This was not the case as Hindus were discriminated and often denied the opportunity to practice their religion while working in the sugar plantations of Natal. In the Hindu religion, in general, worship of Mother Goddess Parvati and Lord Sri Shiva is more common among Hindus of South Indian origin. Hindus of North Indian origin worship Rama, or in the case of

199. *Ibid.*, at 12.
200. *Ibid.*, at 13.
201. A. Taybob, *Islamic Resurgence in South Africa: The Muslim Youth Movement*, 12 Journal of Religion in Africa 104 (2014).
202. *Ibid.*
203. *Ibid.*, at 105.
204. *Ibid.*
205. *Ibid.*, at 106.
206. B. Brain, *Setting Down Roots: Indian Migrants in South Africa, 1890–1911* 12 (Wits University Press 1990).
207. *Ibid.*

Gujaratis, Vishnu.[208] However, it is important to note that there are many similarities among Hindus in South Africa, which ultimately make the Hindu community as a whole.

87. Deepavali is an important festival for the Hindu community in South Africa and is a major attraction of the city of Durban, where different festivals and other festivities are held. The city of Durban is home to the majority of people who follow the Hindu faith and way of life, and that is the reason why this city serves as a hub for the Hindu festival, in most cases.[209]

IV. Jewish Religion

88. The Jewish Religion in South Africa came as a result of the British colonisers in South Africa in 1669, and this was due to the fact that they came for economic opportunities in South Africa at the time, in particular with the discovery of diamond in Johannesburg.[210] Jewish religion is one of the minority religions in South Africa, and the people who subscribe to this form of religion are mainly stationed in the Western Cape province of South Africa.[211] The Jews, like the Christians and Muslims, believe that God created everything and that he is the Lord of the Universe. They further believe that they have an agreement with God as stated in the Bible in which God makes a promise to Abraham and his descendants that he will be their God and they will be his people.[212]

89. There are two Jewish groups: Orthodox and Reformed Jews. Orthodox Jews are the ones who follow the law strictly without any compromise and only worship in Hebrew.[213] While the Reformed Jews, who came into existence in 1800, apply the law with much flexibility, and not strictly. They also worship in Hebrew and make use of their indigenous language when they worship.[214] It is important to note that like all other minority religions in South Africa, the Jews experienced a measure of discrimination, but their discrimination was less hostile and cruel as compared to other minority religious groups like Muslims.[215] This was attributed to the fact that Jews belonged to a white privileged class who looked similar to the oppressors at that time in South Africa.[216]

208. *Ibid.*, at 13.
209. *Ibid.*
210. F.A. Hugh, *South African Jews and Apartheid*, 34 Patterns of Prejudice 23 (2000).
211. *Ibid.*
212. *Ibid.*, at 24.
213. *Ibid.*
214. *Ibid.*, at 25.
215. *Ibid.*
216. *Ibid.*, at 26.

V. African Traditional Religion

90. African beliefs and practices emanate from all aspects of life at the level of both the individual and society. One does not convert into this religion. Everyone in the African society is believed to be born into the religion and thus becomes an active member or participant of a spiritual journey, which originates from the spiritual world and eventually goes back to the spiritual world.[217] It is argued that African religion includes fundamental beliefs, which are common to all Africans, despite the fact that Africa consists of a multitude of nations, with complex cultures and languages.[218] Because of these commonalities based on religion, it is asserted that it must always be spoken in the singular. However, Kiernan holds a different view to the above assertions on the basis that African religion is pluralistic and must be considered like that and not in the singular. This is because it denotes all the indigenous religions in South Africa – not only the faiths of the various black African people but also faiths of people like the San and the Khoi.[219] The term 'indigenous religions' would of course not only apply to South Africa, but it would go beyond and also include the whole of the continent of Africa due to its diverse nature.

91. It is believed that African beliefs and practices originated from the spiritual world, and they were handed down to the physical world by the forbearers by word of mouth, by practical participation in ritual activities and by the day-to-day teachings of the elderly to the children.[220] There is no founder for African religion. This religion was revealed to the first generation, who were directly created by the supernatural power or God. This supernatural being gave to the first generation all laws and taboos on how to live in harmony with God, with other people and nature.[221] People were instructed to marry each other for reproductive purposes, and parents were tasked with the duty to lead their offsprings by example in a manner that will promote good moral values.[222] When the first generation died, their spirits joined the spiritual world where the Creator lives. This marked the beginning of ancestors who became the messengers of the Creator and the supervisors of the physical world.[223] The ancestors looked after the welfare of the living mainly through the elderly, who taught the youth orally and through rituals.[224] In this way, the religion was passed on from one generation to another generation. From time to time, the elders also revealed themselves to the living of all ages through dreams and visions.[225]

217. Mndende, *supra* n. 84, at 40.
218. *Ibid.*
219. *Ibid.*, at 41.
220. *Ibid.*
221. *Ibid.*, at 42.
222. *Ibid.*
223. *Ibid.*, at 43.
224. *Ibid.*
225. *Ibid.*, at 44.

92. African religion can be summarised in five elements according to the assertions that are raised by Oosthuizen. That African religion is a belief in a supreme being; belief in lesser Gods; belief in spirits; ancestral beliefs and the practice of magic and medicine each with its own cult.[226] According to Oosthuizen, these core elements relate with each other because African thinking and practice are always in terms of groups. Everything is part of a group and each individual only makes sense in as far as it is connected with everything else.[227] This would mean that the physical and the spiritual world are very closely connected in African religion.

§3. Conclusion

93. In conclusion, it is important to note that South Africa is made up of people with different religious and cultural beliefs, who make up the South African community, which is generally regarded as pluralistic in nature. Focus will now shift to the freedom and independence of religion and religious practices in South Africa on the individual, collective and organisational basis.

226. *Ibid.*
227. *Ibid.*, at 45.

Part II. Religious Freedom in General

Chapter 1. Individual and Collective Religious Freedom

§1. Introduction

94. Individual and collective religious freedom will be discussed jointly in this chapter. This is because both individual and collective religious freedom cannot be separated based on the following reasons. An individual does not practice a religious or cultural practice alone or in isolation with other people; t for that religious practice or culture to be recognised, it must be done in the collective with other people. This means that the individual freedom, which a person enjoys when it comes to religious and cultural freedom, forms a part of the collective in the practice of that particular religion or culture. Based on these reasons, this chapter will highlight the importance of religious freedom from an individual point of view, which in turn will result to a collective religious freedom, which the particular individual enjoys as protected by the Constitution.

95. Constitutional provisions, which aim to promote the freedom of religion for both an individual and the collective, will be discussed in this chapter. Furthermore, the extent to which a right protects the individual and collective freedom when it comes to religion and cultural practices is explored. The views of various authors in relation to freedom of religion for both an individual and collective are outlined for a comprehensive understanding of the constitutional protection of freedom to religion on both an individual and collective basis.

§2. Constitutional Protection of the Right to Religious Freedom on an Individual and Collective Basis

96. Despite the constitutional protection of religious and cultural freedom in South Africa, it is still difficult to simply define the freedom of religion and culture as a constitutional right. This is because it is much more of a concept that needs to be circumscribed. It is also a concept that can continue to develop in future due to the changing needs of the society. Section 15(1) of the Constitution provides that everyone has the right to freedom of conscience, religion, thought, belief and opinion.[228] It is understood that groups that observe distinctive cultural and religious practices are also guaranteed this freedom of religion and culture on a collective basis. However, they must ensure that their personal laws and customs do not violate the Constitution.[229]

97. This means that primarily it remains the task of the individual and religious groups of South Africa to identify those rights in a way that is consistent with their own religious identity and within the ambit of the Constitution and the laws of the country all the time. If the religions and religious people of South Africa do not accept this role and task it will be taken away from them by government, courts and society and it will be done in a way which will not necessarily further freedom of religion, and this can be returning to the previous era of colonialism and apartheid.[230] In the era of colonialism and apartheid religious freedom was not in existence as people were prohibited at some point to take part in a religious practice of their choice, and let alone they could not be in a position to choose the religion or cultural practice of their choice. Briefly, this means that in the new constitutional dispensation in fulfilling their task, churches and cultural groups must make sure of their deep roots and identity and make sure of the rights and obligations that spring from those roots and identity. They must also take note of the Bill of Rights as contained in the second chapter of the Constitution, as well as the Acts of parliaments, which further describe the content and application of the rights concerned.[231]

§3. The Extent of the Right to Freedom of Religion on an Individual and Collective Basis

98. While section 15(1) of the Constitution guarantees the right of every person to belief or hold an opinion,[232] subsection 15(3) of the Constitution draws a distinction between freedom of belief, on the one hand, and the right to practice such belief or religion on the other.[233] This section indirectly restricts the right of any person to practice his or her religion or culture. Section 15(3) (a) of the Constitution states that this provision does not prevent legislation recognising (i) marriages concluded under any tradition, or a system of religious, personal or family law; or (ii) systems of personal and family law under any tradition, or adhered to by persons professing a particular religion.[234] Section 15(1) (a) of the Constitution can best be described as a negative right as opposed to a positive right on the basis that there is no compulsion on the part of the legislature to legally recognise religious practices and religious law. Instead, the legislature has a choice not to pass any law at all that will recognise religious practices or law.

228. Section 15(1) of the Constitution.
229. Section 36 of the Constitution.
230. Mndende, *supra* n. 84, at 43.
231. Section 2 of the Constitution.
232. Section 15(1) of the Constitution.
233. Section 15(3) of the Constitution.
234. Section 15(3) (a) of the Constitution.

99. It is argued that the constitutional protection of freedom of conscience, religion, thought, belief and opinion only protects the religious belief, but it does not recognise the observance of the rules of religion, which is religious laws. What is actually not protected by this provision is the practice associated with the recognition of religious law. In most instances, belief and practice cannot be separated because belief leads to the practice based on that belief. It is absurd to have any other interpretation of section 15 of the Constitution other than to conclude that this provision, read with sections 15(2) and (3) of the Constitution, guarantees both the freedom of belief and the freedom to practice that religion.[235] This conclusion is based on two reasons: section 15(3) of the Constitution automatically prohibits any religious law or practice of religion that violates any provision in the Constitution. Although this provision seems unnecessary since it is a repetition of the supremacy clause of the Constitution as per section 2, its purpose seems to be to ensure that the legislature will not codify unconstitutional religious law.[236] The point is that this provision obviously does not affect the constitutional recognition of any religious belief or practice of religious law that is not contrary to the Constitution.

100. Furthermore, section 15(3) of the Constitution also seems unnecessary because it does not assist in the protection of religious freedom, but simply provides that the legislature may not be prevented by any other law from recognising systems of religious or personal law. That is, the correct interpretation of section 15 of the Constitution is that freedom of religious beliefs and freedom to practice any law associated with any such religion or belief should be regarded as protected by the Constitution.[237] Consequently, all aspects of religious law, such as Christian laws and Jewish laws among others, currently form a part or should be regarded as forming a part of the South African legal system where they are not inconsistent with the Constitution.[238] When interpreting the common law, courts should interpret section 15 of the Constitution to include both the right to freedom of belief and the right to practice that belief.[239] Any other interpretation will defeat the objectives of this provision. The current attitudes of the courts when interpreting section 15 of the Constitution is considered below. It will be exposed that courts are not in favour of adopting a liberal interpretation by protecting both belief and practice of that belief according to the principles of the relevant personal laws, even if those personal laws do not violate the Bill of Rights.

235. Section 15(2) and (3) of the Constitution.
236. Section 15(3) of the Constitution.
237. Section 15(1) of the Constitution.
238. Section 36 of the Constitution.
239. Section 39 of the Constitution.

§4. The Attitudes and Conduct of the South African Courts While Interpreting Freedom of Religion on an Individual and Collective Basis

101. If the above interpretation to freedom of religion in South Africa is correct, why do South African courts continue to refuse to legally recognise and enforce religious laws, in particular, to legally recognise religious marriages? The interpretation clause in the Constitution according to section 39(1)[240] obliges courts to promote the values that underlie an open and democratic society based on human dignity, equality and freedom and to promote the spirit, purport and objects of the Bill of Rights. For example, African and Muslim religions as well as customary law do not share the same prestige and protection that is afforded to civil law in matters that concern the protection of human rights. Cleary the courts have come to realise the inconsistencies in their application of the Bill of Rights pertaining to personal laws which include religious laws. Despite this realisation, the courts have constantly refused to legalise religious marriages. In *Ryland v. Edros*,[241] the court had to consider whether public policy depended on the views of the majority Christian religion under the current constitutional dispensation. The court in this case concluded by outlining that it is quite inimical to all the values of the new South Africa that the courts should only brand a Muslim marriage contract as offensive to public policy. It is offensive and a regress to the democratic South Africa, which is diverse and pluralistic in nature.[242]

102. Despite this observation, the courts still refused to give legal recognition to Islamic marriages. Similarly, in holding that the consequences of any contract resulting from an invalid Muslim marriage may be recognised under certain circumstances, the court in *Amod v. Khan*[243] held that the new Constitution ushered in a new value system based on equality, religious freedom and dignity as opposed to the *boni mores* of society.[244] In this case, Mahomed CJ held that:

> the insistence that the duty of support which such serious de facto monogamous marriage imposes on the husband is not worthy of protection, can only be justified on the basis that the only duty of support which the law will protect in such circumstances is a duty following from a marriage solemnised and recognised by one faith or philosophy to the exclusion of others. This is an untenable basis for the determination of the *boni mores* of society. It is inconsistent with the new ethos of tolerance, pluralism and religious freedom which had consolidated itself in the community even before the formal adoption of the interim Constitution on 22 December 1993.[245]

240. Section 39(1) of the Constitution.
241. *Ryland v. Edros* 1997 (2) SA 690 (CC).
242. *Ibid.*
243. *Amod v. Khan* 1947 (2) SA 432 (N).
244. *Ibid.*, at 433.
245. *Ibid.*

103. Furthermore, in this case the court expressly refused to recognise Islamic marriages. The reasons why courts in South Africa do not recognise and enforce religious marriages and laws were revealed in *Ismail v. Ismail.*[246] In this case, the court had to decide whether the consequences of a Muslim marriage, which is still legally unrecognised because it is regarded as potentially polygamous and therefore contrary to public policy, could be legally enforced upon, divorce.[247] Judge Van Reenen in this case held that:

> The marriage law of the State is rooted in Christianity whereas the union of plaintiff and defendant is based on a non-Christian faith. At the advent of Protestantism, marriage was secularised and passed under the control of the State. However, although as a result of the advent of Protestantism marriage was secularised, the countries of the Reformed Church retained the idea of its being of divine institution in its general origin.[248]

104. It is important to note that this case was decided ten years before the adoption of the Constitution and the Bill of Rights in South Africa, yet the courts have consistently refused to recognise religious marriage law other than Christian marriages, even in the new constitutional dispensation. Immediately after the Interim Constitution came into operation, the court in *Marais v. The Master* held that potentially polygamous marriages might contravene the gender equality principle on the following basis.[249] Apart from that, the principle of gender equality embodied in sections 8(2) and 119(3) in the Constitution and constitutional principles stated in section 232(4) may well lead to the conclusion that polygamous marriages are as unacceptable to the *boni mores* of the new South Africa as they were to the old.[250] Another problem as outlined above is that in *Amod v. Khan* the court consciously refused to deal with the issue of the validity of a Muslim religious marriage under the current constitutional dispensation, arguing that the duty of spouse support does not depend on the validity of a marriage.[251] The court held that, for the purposes of the dependant's action, the decisive issue is not whether the dependant concerned was or was not lawfully married to the deceased, but whether or not the deceased was under a legal duty to support the dependant in a relationship, which deserved recognition and protection as per common law.[252]

105. From the above assessments and court cases it is clear that courts have an important role to fulfil in order to ensure that fundamental rights are upheld and protected. This is unfortunately not yet the case as outlined, particularly when dealing with freedom of religion on an individual and collective basis. Focus from a constitutional perspective will now shift to a statutory law perspective when it comes to the position of freedom of religion on an individual and collective basis.

---

246. *Ismail v. Ismail* 1983 1 SA 1006 (W).
247. *Ibid.*
248. *Ibid.*, at 1007.
249. *Marais v. The Master* 1984 (4) SH 288 (D).
250. *Ibid.*
251. *Amod v. Khan, supra* n. 1 at 434.
252. *Ibid.*

§5. The Position of the Charter of Religious Rights and Freedom in Individual and Collective Freedom to Religion

106. The charter, as it was discussed above, as one of the instruments in South Africa that serves to promote and protect freedom of religion in line with the Constitution also puts provisions in place that ensure that the freedom of religion on an individual and collective basis is upheld. This includes making the following provisions without getting into the detail:

(a) The right to believe or not to believe.
(b) The obligations of the state with regard to religious rights.
(c) The right to observe and exercise one's religion.
(d) The right to education consistent with one's religious convictions.
(e) The right to maintain particular matrimonial, family and personal legal traditions.
(f) The right to institutional freedom.
(g) The rights and obligations of religion with regard to the laws of the land.
(h) The right of religion to freedom of expression.
(i) The right of religion to freedom of association.
(j) The right of religion to freedom of propagation.
(k) The right to religious dignity.
(l) The right of religion to solicit, receive, manage and spend voluntary financial and other forms of support and contributions.
(m) The right of religion to conduct upliftment and charity work in the community and to establish, maintain and contribute to charity and welfare associations, and solicit, manage, distribute and spend funds for this purpose.

107. All of the above in fact describes what freedom of religion on an individual and collective basis entails. It can also be said in the words of John Witte as he argues that freedom of religion includes:

(1) freedom of conscience;
(2) the free exercise of religion;
(3) religious pluralism;
(4) religious equality;
(5) the separation of church and state; and
(6) the disestablishment of religion by the state.[253]

108. From the above provisions it is apparent and clear that religious freedom on an individual and collective basis is firmly entrenched in the charter in conjunction with the Constitution as the supreme law of the land in South Africa. However, as already pointed out, from the perspective of the constitutional law and protection in relation to freedom of religion there is a problem with regard to the interpretation

253. Section 2 of the South African Charter of Religious Rights and Freedom.

and application of this provision. A liberal approach in connection with the interpretation and application of freedom of religion on an individual and collective basis is essential. It should not rely on *boni mores* as a limiting factor because the only way a fundamental right can be limited in a just and fair manner is through the application of section 36 of the Constitution as the general limitation clause.[254]

§6. Conclusion

109. Considering all the issues discussed above, one is bound to conclude that the South African courts have failed to promote the values that underlie an open and democratic society based on human dignity, equality and freedom.[255] Furthermore, the courts have failed to promote the spirit, purport and objects of the Bill of Rights by not recognising that religious personal law have become part of the mainstream legal system in South Africa. The courts have failed to protect the right of different people to practice their religion by not recognising that the right to freedom of religion includes not only the mental aspects of belief but also freedom to practice and have legal protection of the rules of that religion.

110. By favouring the rules of the Christian faith, the courts have unfairly discriminated against other religions. To rectify this mistake, and to deal with such problems in a free and democratic society based on freedom and fundamental human rights, the legislature must develop laws to reflect legal diversity and legal pluralism as contemplated in section 15 of the Constitution. Different laws have different functions to fulfil, functions for which they are best suited, and this view is supported because it includes or accommodates for diversity, which is the South African position. Other laws need not of necessity be in conflict with state laws; they may complement state laws and direct the development of state laws in harmony with basic values underlying non-state legal and social systems. Clearly, there is a need for recognition of legal pluralism concerning matters of private law. This would comply with the right to freedom of religion as guaranteed in the Constitution, considering the fact that everyone has a right to follow a religion of his or her choice, either as an individual or as a collective.

254. Section 36 of the Constitution.
255. Section 2 of the Constitution.

Chapter 2. Organisational Religious Freedom

§1. Introduction

111. Freedom of religion and culture as protected and enshrined in both the Constitution and legislation means that different religious organisations as well as cultural organisations have the freedom to practice and uphold their religion and culture. These organisations in the South African context refer to churches, synagogues and mosques due to the diverse and pluralistic nature of the South African community. Furthermore, it will also refer to the cultural groups or associations of the different indigenous communities and societies. The freedom to practice religion and cultural practices that is vested with the churches and cultural associations means that these organisations are free to determine how their churches and cultural groups must operate in realising their faith or belief in the process. However, this must be done in such a way that it does not infringe any rights or is not contrary to the Constitution as the supreme law of the land.

112. In this chapter focus will be placed on how faith-based organisations in South Africa are free to determine their administrative position in realising individual and collective rights to freedom of religion and culture.

§2. The South African Charter of Religious Rights and Freedoms

113. Section 9 of the charter provides that religious organisations are subject to the rule of law in South Africa, despite the freedom that is guaranteed to them for religion and cultural practice.[256] The charter accepts the reality that religious organisations exist and function within society, are therefore a part of society, and that in principle they are therefore subject to the law. As a matter of fact, a religious organisation carries a particular responsibility to teach its members good citizenship and the importance of observing the law in the interest of society as a whole for the common good.[257] A religious organisation may also not act in a way that is blatantly illegal, for example to force its members to perform acts or rituals that are physically harmful or may damage or destroy the property of others or to force minors to marry. This will be found to be contrary to the Constitution and such practices will be declared null and void to such an extent that criminal prosecution will have to be carried out.[258]

114. However, if a religious organisation, while exercising the rights guaranteed in the charter in a lawful way, feels it cannot in good conscience observe a particular law, it must be able to justify itself on the ground that it is inconsistent with its beliefs and convictions as guaranteed by the Constitution.[259] Sometimes a law may

256. Section 9 of the South African Charter of Religious Rights and Freedom.
257. *Ibid.*
258. Section 2 of the Constitution.
259. Section 15 of the Constitution.

even contain exemptions on religious grounds, precisely to accommodate those who disagree based on their beliefs or convictions. An example is the Civil Union Act, which provides that religious marriage officers must not be compelled to solemnise marriages between persons of same sex.[260] The approach followed in this provision does not imply that a religious institution or its leaders may break the law. The right to not observe a particular law, with which one disagrees, is not a licence for illegal behaviour.

115. Similarly, it is necessary to recall that diversity depends upon difference being respected and that law should not be used as a means of homogenising society. There are those who wish everyone to believe as they do on matters where we should allow differences of opinion and this is mostly the case in relation to terror attacks like the Boko Haram group in Nigeria.[261] Maintaining a space for difference of beliefs – sometimes on matters that are deeply held by those who believe otherwise, particularly in relation to political issues on the day and on matters like sexual orientation, gender rights or religious beliefs – however, is one of the marks of a mature and respectful society and a recognition of law understood within its proper bounds. Due to the importance of diversity in relation to freedom of persons, organisations and society itself, the onus should be on those who wish to challenge the presumption of diversity to show legal regulation and restriction is necessary and in the public interest. The hurdle for such a rebuttal should be significant since the dignity and freedom of difference is what is at stake.

§3. Independence of Religious Organisations in South Africa

116. Section 9(2) of the charter deals with the duty of the state to respect, protect, promote and facilitate the right to religious freedom of organisations in South Africa as protected by the Constitution.[262] The state must recognise the authority of religious organisations over their own affairs, and the state must govern justly, constructively and impartially in the interest of everybody. Recognition of a legal presumption in favour of diversity and the limits of law in relation to internal matters of religion alongside generally applicable principles of procedural fairness and natural justice are important to achieve justice, fairness and respect for difference within a constitutional order such as South Africa.[263] Developing legal recognition of how these principles interact is an aspect of the evolution of both legal and societal maturity and a rejection of the domination of the past.

260. Section 33 of the Civil Union Act 2004.
261. *Nigeria's Boko Haram*, https://www.bbc.com/news/world-africa-31784538 (accessed 9 Aug. 2018).
262. Section 9(2) of the South African Charter of Religious Rights and Freedom.
263. *Ibid.*

117. Furthermore, section 9(3) of the charter deals with the internal religious matters which are free from the state and the courts in as far as religious organisations are concerned.[264] In this aspect, the charter puts emphasis on the important consequence of the independence of religious organisations, in that the state, including the courts, may not regulate or prescribe matters concerning religious confessions, doctrines and ordinances. This actually reflects the long-standing principle in the law that the state should not make laws on religious matters, and courts should not decide cases of religious confessions, doctrines and ordinances.[265] This is because matters of religious doctrine, confessions and ordinances are not matters over which courts may rightly claim jurisdiction, as they have no expertise in relation to religious revelations. In addition, should courts delve into this area, they would diminish the independence that religious organisations are free and independent from the state interference. This will mean that there will be an overreach on the part of the courts because they would enter into an area of religious dogma, which is something beyond the proper purview of the law.

§4. Assessment of Religious Organisation's Freedom and Independence in South Africa

I. Christian Faith

118. Despite the challenges, which were outlined above when it comes to the interpretation of the freedom to religion by the courts in South Africa from a constitutional point of view. It is noted that churches are still able to develop their own rules and procedures in order to realise and enjoy the freedom of religion, which is guaranteed by the Constitution and the charter as outlined. The Christian faith is the majority in South Africa and comprises of different churches or organisations with different distinctive features and practices. However, despite their differences they share a common element or factor, which is they are all the followers of Christ who is the Saviour of humankind.[266] The head of the church will normally be the reverend or a pastor and will be assisted by a group of elders, which is normally called the church council. The church council will play a very important role when it comes to the day-to-day operations of the church and advice the minister or pastor on key strategic decisions which need to be taken or followed by the church for it to grow and be sustainable.

119. Because the Christian faith is the largest in South Africa, reference will be made in this study to one church organisation with the aim of showing the independence and freedom, which religious organisations enjoy in South Africa from the perspective of both a constitutional and statutory law. For example, the Methodist Church of Southern Africa is one of the churches that came to South Africa through

264. Section 9(3) of the South African Charter of Religious Rights and Freedom.
265. *Ibid.*
266. Holy Bible 2 Corinthians Ch 5: Verses 14.

the missionary work and intervention during the colonial era. This church as a religious organisation enjoys freedom and independence, which is upheld and protected by both the Constitution and the charter. The Methodist Church has its own Constitution as a church, which is Laws and Disciplines of the Methodist Church of Southern Africa (L&D). L&D prescribes how the church must be run on a daily basis and how congregants must behave in church and what they must wear as a way of representing the broader church.[267] Furthermore, L&D prescribes how office bearers are appointed and elected in the church and outline how these office bearers must execute their role and functions in the process.[268]

120. The development of an instrument like the L&D affirms that religious organisations are autonomous in South Africa and independent from state interference in realising a fundamental right such as freedom to religion and cultural practices. The same can be said with other churches in South Africa like Roman Catholic Church, Lutheran and Dutch Reformed Church among others. They are in a position to develop their own internal rules and processes in such a way that it will govern how they operate in South Africa in harmony and peace with other faith-based organisations.[269] This religious freedom, which the Christian faith enjoys despite their majority status in South Africa, does not mean that they are given a blanket clause to develop rules that are contrary to the rule of law in South Africa or to divide society by formulating discrimination rules. In such cases, the Constitution as the supreme law of the land will be the one that reigns supreme and such rule or practice of the religious organisation will be declared void.[270]

II. Muslim Faith

121. When it comes to the Muslim faith or religion, the mosques are considered as independent religious organisations and have rules and standards, which form part of the Muslim religion and tradition, which in a sense sets them apart from other religious organisations. In the mosques, normally a prayer leader is a person that is well respected among the congregants, and he leads a productive and honest lifestyle. Members of the congregants will vote for the prayer leader.[271] Since a mosque is regarded as a place of worship, cleanliness and respect is championed among congregants at all times with the aim of keeping the peace and stability in the mosque. Proper dress code in which long clothes that do not reveal any part of the body is prescribed, and women to further cover their heads is encouraged because anything that is contrary to this will be viewed as disrespectful.[272] As per

267. Z. Siwa, *The Laws and Disciplines of the Methodist Church of Southern Africa* 2 (Methodist Publishing House 12 ed. 2016).
268. *Ibid.*, at 3.
269. Section 15 of the Constitution.
270. Section 2 of the Constitution.
271. Taybob, *supra* n. 202, at 110.
272. *Ibid.*

the sitting arrangement in the mosque, women will sit behind men and that is the tradition of the Muslim religion since ancient times.[273]

III. Hindu Faith

122. Just like other faith-based organisations, Hindus have they own rules and traditions when it comes to observing their faith. The Hindus make use of the temple as a place of worship or assembly and study among other things.[274] The head priest, as the spiritual leader, will be the one who leads the prayers in most cases and when it comes to the sitting arrangement men and women would sit in separate areas. Before entering the temple, it is a standard practice that all congregants must remove their shoes as a sign of showing respect and honour in the temple.[275]

123. When it comes to reform, Hindu faith, which came into existence from the 1,800, holds a different view from the standard practice of the ancient Hindu-based doctrines and practices.[276] According to the reformed Hindu practice, they have introduced musical instruments and a choir to assist with the fellowship in the temple. Furthermore, the practice and rule that congregants when they enter into the temple must remove their shoes has been removed and is no longer in operation, and the rule that men and women must sit in separate places does no longer apply, which was the position in the ancient Hindu religion.[277] With the reformed Hindu faith, it is clear that the position in terms of their doctrine and rules, they follow a format that is similar to that of a church which is a place of worship for the Christian faith.

IV. Jewish Faith

124. In the case of the Jews, they make use of a synagogue as a place of worship to God. Like other religious groups, the Jewish religion is also autonomous when it comes to formulating rules and regulations in connection with how a member or congregant of the Jewish religion must behave.[278] Most of these rules or regulations emanate from the Jewish traditions or the way of life, for example if a boy child has been born, then such a child must go for circumcision on the eighth day of his birth for him to be welcomed to the Jewish community and religion.[279] This is attributed to the fact that it is in line with the convenant made with God and the people of Israel.

273. *Ibid.*, at 111.
274. Brain, *supra* n. 207, at 13.
275. Ibid., at 14.
276. *Ibid.*
277. *Ibid.*
278. Hugh, *supra* n. 211, at 30.
279. *Ibid.*

125. The Jews when they enter the synagogue there are also rules and procedures which they need to observe as a sign of showing respect and honour in the synagogue. For example, the congregants must wear a kippah, which traditionally only men are permitted to wear, but due to the reform, women can also wear it.[280] In addition, a prayer leader is also in charge in leading the congregants during prayer sessions as a Shepard of God.[281]

V. African Customary Faith

126. When it comes to African faith there is a common element between all indigenous groups or cultural affiliations. The most common denominator is the fact that there is a belief in the ancestors who are the messengers of God.[282] In the African faith ancestors play an important role in the lives of the indigenous community to such an extent that great respect is bestowed on the graveside. People must wear in an appropriate manner when they enter the graveyard; for example, men must wear a jacket and women must wear a dress or skirt but cannot wear a trouser, as that will be viewed as disrespectful and contrary to the public interests.[283] Furthermore, it is a standard practice among the indigenous communities that one cannot speak ill about the dead because they play an important role when it comes to the development and up keep of society.[284]

127. In terms of African faith it is important to bear in mind that the practice of appeasing the ancestors is key and this includes the ceremony of slaughtering a cow, goat, sheep and chicken as well as brewing African beer as all these will serve as sacrifices to the ancestors.[285] Sacrifices are made to pray for rain or to welcome a new season as a way of expressing gratitude, or requesting for intervention to the ancestors and God for prosperity and development in society. When performing African cultural practices or religion, normally these ceremonies will be performed at a certain place which is earmarked as sacred by the family or community which is similar to churches in the Christian faith or a synagogue in the Jewish faith.[286] The spiritual leader in the African culture will normally be a traditional healer who is the mouthpiece of the ancestors, and in some instances, the eldest member of the family can lead this ceremony. This can include the uncle or aunt who both play a vital role in African culture due to their bloodline and position in the cultural context.[287] This means that it is not everyone who can play the role of a spiritual leader when it comes to the aspect of African religion.

---

280. *Ibid.*, at 31.
281. *Ibid.*
282. Mndende, *supra* n. 84, at 18.
283. *Ibid.*
284. *Ibid.*, at 19.
285. *Ibid.*
286. *Ibid.*, at 20.
287. *Ibid.*

128. There are also processes and rules that need to be observed when it comes to practising African religion with the aim of ensuring that this religion is maintained and preserved for generations to come. For example, initiation of young boys is a cultural practice that is observed to mean that one moves from a stage of being a boy to the stage of being a man. During this practice only old men are permitted to perform and guide these young boys, and this practice happens in the mountains during the winter season and no woman is permitted to enter or be part of this practice. As such an interference by a woman during this cultural practice will be a taboo and a violation of this ancient and prestigious cultural practice of the indigenous community.

§5. Conclusion

129. Without a doubt in South Africa freedom of religion from an individual, collective and organisational perspective is upheld and protected by the Constitution and statutory instruments. However, there is still a problem with the interpretation of this fundamental right by the courts as outlined, but this does not take away the autonomy and independence which religious and cultural organisations enjoy as outlined above. The autonomy of the various religious and cultural organisations in South Africa, which make up the pluralistic society, can formulate rules and procedures that govern their operations with the aim of realising their right to freedom of religion and independence. This is not an absolute power, in the sense that these religious and cultural organisations can't do as they please and violate the rights of other people. Such conduct will be viewed as unlawful and void in terms of the Constitution as the supreme law of the land.

130. Religious organisations, despite their independence and freedom, are still subject to the rule of law and must comply and uphold the supremacy of the Constitution in their internal regulations and processes. Regarding the independence and freedom of religion and practice, from an organisational point of view, attention will now be on the recognition and position of religious societies in South Africa in the next chapters.

Part III. Legal Status of Religious Communities

Chapter 1. Formal Status and Autonomy of Religious Communities

§1. Introduction

131. In South Africa, various religious and cultural practices are recognised and upheld, which make up the South African community. As already outlined in the previous chapters, freedom of religion and culture are firmly entrenched and protected in South Africa from a number of vantage points, and this includes from an individual, collective and organisational perspective. The question that now arises is does this freedom and independence to choose religion and culture stretch beyond the above-mentioned constitutional perspectives to such an extent that it gives rise to the protection and promotion of a religious and cultural community in existence in South Africa.

132. This chapter aims to interrogate if there is a recognition of religious and cultural communities in South Africa and if so to what extent, bearing in mind the freedom that is afforded to religion and culture from an individual, collective and organisational point of view. Furthermore, it will be argued whether the freedom to choose and practice religion and culture from these different perspectives ultimately gives rise to the promotion and development of the various religious and cultural communities, and if so, are religious and cultural communities afforded the necessary legal status and protection by the Constitution. Furthermore, this chapter aims to interrogate the legal position and independence of religious and cultural communities in South Africa. The legal status and independence of religious and cultural communities cannot be separated because they relate with each other to a lesser or greater extent.

§2. Constitutional Position on Religious Communities

133. Section 31(1) of the Constitution states that persons belonging to a cultural, religious or linguistic community may not be denied the right, with the other members of that community: (a) to enjoy their culture, practice their religion and use their language; (b) to form, join and maintain cultural, religious and linguistic associations and other organs of civil society.[288] Furthermore, section 31(2) of the Constitution states that the rights mentioned in section 31(1) above may not be exercised in a manner that is found to be inconsistent with the provisions of the Bill of Rights.[289]

134. From the above assessment of this constitutional provision, it is clear that religious and cultural organisations can indeed form a part of a religious or cultural community and the common denominator in the formulation of that community or society will be the religion or culture. However, in the formulation of religious or cultural community through religion or culture it is important to bear in mind that such a religious or cultural community is still subject to the rule of law and the supremacy of the Constitution in South Africa. This means that despite the autonomy to formulate their own rules and procedures from an organisational point of view as well as from a communal point of view, for example, in setting out standards of living for the members of their community they are still subject to the rule of law. What this means is that a religious or cultural community cannot exercise its rights and powers in a manner that it undermines the Constitution to such an extent that the rights of other people who do not form part of that religious or cultural community are compromised. Hence section 31(2) of the Constitution serves as a cautionary clause to section 31(1) of the Constitution, which encourages religious and cultural communities to be formed.

135. It is important for the reader to bear in mind that despite the recognition and encouragement by the Constitution on the formulation of religious and cultural communities, it does not mean that these communities operate in isolation from the state. They are autonomous to such an extent to realise and uphold their religion and culture as protected by the Constitution.[290] This means that religious and cultural communities are not independent states or communities in South Africa who can operate in parallel to the state or to even compete with the state, but these religious and cultural communities form part of the government, and in executing their daily role are required to champion the interests of the government. The recognition of religious and cultural communities in South Africa, with their diversity, aims to bring and achieve the necessary social cohesion without paying attention to the difference or diversity that are identified in the various religious and cultural communities. Religious and cultural communities play an important role in building the society of South Africa because among other things, which the law cannot be, they are able to instil values and good manners on people to relate with each other in a respectful and dignified manner. They teach members values like respect, tolerance, compassion and solidarity, which form part of the African concept of *Ubuntu, botho*, as one of the values that underpin our Constitutional democracy.[291]

288. Section 31(1) of the Constitution.
289. Section 31(2) of the Constitution.
290. Section 31(1) of the Constitution.
291. G.J. Van Niekerk & L. Wildenboer, *The Origins of South African Law* 177 (UNISA 2010).

136. In the African culture, maintaining peace and social relations is important for the survival and growth of society in which emphasis is not placed on the individual but on the broader community as a whole.[292] This principle is embedded in the African concept of *Ubuntu,* which is a normative source of indigenous law and implies coexistence of human rights and freedoms, on the one hand, and collective duties, on the other hand. It places emphasis on the role of the individual as a member of the community.[293] Furthermore, *Ubuntu* implies a spirit of humanness and includes virtues such as compassion, forgiveness and human dignity.[294] *Ubuntu*, as an indigenous law source, was recognised in *S v. Makwanyane*,[295] where the Constitutional Court was of the view that in interpreting the Bill of Rights, indigenous values ought to be put to effect, and thus develop a specific South African understanding of human rights and indigenous law as a system of law in our country.

137. Religious and cultural communities in addition to instilling values and good behaviour on their members are also important in other factors. They hold a position of trust and confidence among their members. This means that they can be in a position to reach to their members with efficiency and help their members to deal with other personal and spiritual issues, which in most instances can fall beyond the powers of the state.[296] This relationship of trust cannot be underestimated because it is influential and gives power to the religious and cultural organisations. That is the reason why it is said that religious and cultural communities are obliged to promote the interest of the state to their members because they hold the position of trust and confidence.

138. Reference will now be made to the various religious and cultural communities that are recognised in South Africa in their diversity. Furthermore, the role and practice of these religious and cultural communities will be explored, and how they use their position of trust from the point of a religious or cultural community with the aim of ensuring that democracy in South Africa is strengthened and upheld will be interrogated.

§3. Recognised Religious and Cultural Communities in South Africa

139. South Africa is a multi-faceted and rainbow nation due to the various religious and cultural communities that make up the South African population. For this discussion, reference will not be made to all religious and cultural communities that are recognised in South Africa, but the discussion will be restricted to two of these religious and cultural communities. The reason for this limitation is on the basis that all religious and cultural communities share a common element, which is to bring

292. C. Gibbs, *Recent Developments Regarding South African Common Law and Customary Law of Succession* 23 (University of Pretoria Press 2015).
293. Van Niekerk and Wildenboer, *supra* n. 292, at 177.
294. *Ibid.*, at 178.
295. *S v. Makwanyane* 1995 (6) BCLR 6655 (CC).
296. *A Gross Abuse of a Position of Trust*, https://www.churchtimes.co.uk/articles/2016/9-december/comment/opinion/tackling-abuse-on-pitch-and-pulpit (accessed 17 Aug. 2018).

the necessary social cohesion through the process of instilling discipline and respect among its members and the broader community.

140. The Christian community, which is the leading religious domination in South Africa, will be discussed, and it will be outlined how this religious community share similarity with other religious communities that are recognised in South Africa. The cultural community of the indigenous people of South Africa who are governed by African customary law will be discussed, and the discussion about the different tribes or clans in terms of sharing the same identity like *Ubuntu* will be explored in the process.

I. The Christian Community

141. When it comes to the Christian community, it is important to note that South Africans are a very religious people. The question that arises is what is the influence and role of Christians in the South African society? In answering this question it is important to consider this important aspect because trust plays an important role in a democratic society as it consolidates the society and its institutions.[297] Christians are organised in churches as denominations and congregations, and churches appear consistently to enjoy the highest level of trust across the country, with four out of five South Africans indicating that they strongly trust churches.[298] Institutions that are at the bottom of the relative levels of trust in South Africa are the police and labour unions due to the levels of corruption and fraud, which is dominating particularly in state institutions.[299]

142. This places the church and its membership in an important position to have an influence on the South African society. The majority of the population of South Africans believe that there is a God, most members of the Christian community engage in prayers twice or three times a day on average and this is a practice that is instilled in young children and the broader Christian community. What is also championed in this community is honesty in dealing with the state, and this relates to tax compliance and accessing of social grants. In the case of tax compliance the Christian community is expected to encourage their members that in addition to paying their offerings to church as stated in the Holy Bible, they are still obliged to honour their commitment to the state and pay their taxes on time and with diligence.[300] Failure to do so will amount to a serious violation of both state laws and the Christian way of life in which honesty and integrity is central and fundamental. Furthermore, the Christian community also discourages its members from engaging in illegal activities of defrauding the state like accessing social grants even though they do no need it as this is an un-Christ like conduct and is infringing the laws of

297. *Churches and Government Likely to Abuse Trust,* https://www.benkhumalo-seegelken.de/suedafrika-aktuell/1753-church-and-government/ (accessed 30 Sep. 2018).

298. *Ibid.*

299. *Ibid.*

300. W.J. Schoeman, *South African Religious Demography: The 2013 General Household Survey* 4 Theological Studies 2 (2017).

the land.[301] These two examples show and confirm the relationship between the state and the Christian community in working together for ensuring that the necessary social cohesion is being maintained.

143. Christians hold strong orthodox views in relation to the Christian belief or doctrine, and they believe in God and in the Bible as the literal word of God. Jesus is the solution to all of the world's problems.[302] The Christian community has conservative views on support for capital punishment and oppose abortion. In this case, for instance, when it comes to capital punishment the state has taken the position of the Christian community on the basis that only God is the one that gives and takes away life and no man is empowered to take life.[303] This was deliberated in the landmark court case of *S v. Makwanyane*, post-democracy in which a discussion about the abolishment of capital punishment was considered and abandoned.[304] In this case, the highest court of the land held that capital punishment was inhumane, degrading, cruel and contrary to the provisions of the Bill of Rights. This practice was declared unconstitutional in South Africa because it was not in line with the spirit, purpose and objects of the Constitution.[305]

144. This court case and the abolishment of this practice in the South African context affirmed the relationship between the state and the Christian community and with the other religious communities in ensuring that capital punishment is abolished in the new democratic dispensation. The aim in this case was to ensure that the rule of law is upheld in South Africa and that the value of upholding and not taking life from the perspective of a religious community is realised at the same time. However, not all the time will the state and the Christian community agree on everything, for example as already mentioned abortion is prohibited in the Christian community but it is a practice that is recognised as lawful in South Africa.[306] Section 10 of the Constitution states that everyone has inherent dignity and the right to have their dignity respected and protected.[307] Furthermore, it is important to enquire what human dignity means. It is defined as how an individual or group feels, its self-respect and self-worth. Human dignity is concerned with physical and psychological integrity and empowerment and is harmed or violated by unfair treatment premised upon personal traits or circumstances, which do not relate to individual needs, capacities or merits. The right to human dignity is enhanced by laws, which are sensitive to the needs, capacities and merits of different individuals, taking into account the context of their differences.[308] The right to human dignity is harmed or violated when people are marginalised, ignored or devalued, and it is enhanced when laws recognise the full place of all individuals and groups within society.

---

301. *Ibid.*, at 3.
302. Holy Bible Hebrews Ch 2: Verses 14.
303. *S v. Makwanyane*, *supra* n. 296, at 6655.
304. *Ibid.*, at 6656.
305. *Ibid.*
306. Section 2 Choice on Termination of Pregnancy Act 92 of 1997.
307. Section 10 of the Constitution.
308. Schoeman, *supra* n. 301, at 4.

145. The legalisation of a practice like abortion on the part of the state is to realise the fundamental right, which is the right to human dignity, and bodily integrity, which a person enjoys in a democratic society. However, the state still encourages good behaviour and practices among its citizens, while at the same time bearing in mind that, for example, a young child can be raped and be pregnant and must be afforded the opportunity to terminate the pregnancy if they so choose. The socio-economic needs or circumstances can also be a factor when it comes to the termination of pregnancy and the right of the woman who chooses to do so must be respected and upheld as protected by the Constitution.[309] Another important aspect to be considered when it comes to the termination of pregnancy for its legalisation in South Africa is that it was attributed to the fact that many people, in particular young girls, were opting for illegal abortions which was not safe and this resulted in millions of lives lost in the process.[310] The state had to act in the public interest and to stop this practice from escalating and this resulted in the adoption of the Choice on Termination of Pregnancy Act in South Africa, with the aim of legalising adoption. It is clear that when acting in the public interest the state can differ with a religious community about a particular point of view and while at the same time ensuring that the rule of law is upheld and protected.

146. The foundation of Christian communities when dealing with the state is honesty and integrity with the aim of ensuring that the necessary social cohesion is upheld and achieved. The Christian community also instils values and principles to their members as to how they are expected to relate with each other and other people on a daily basis. These include the Ten Commandments in the Bible, which read as follows: You shall not have any other gods before me; you shall not make any idols; you shall not take the name of the Lord your God in vain; remember the Sabbath day, to keep it holy; honour your father and mother; you shall not murder; you shall not commit adultery; you shall not steal; you shall not bear false witness and you shall not covet.[311]

147. These values form part of the Christian community and other religious communities. It can be argued that these values like not to steal, lie, commit murder among others form part of the criminal justice system of South Africa and a person who commits these offences can either be imprisoned or fined. This is in addition to being condemned from a religious community on the basis that a person who does not uphold and respect the Ten Commandments is a sinner who needs the grace of God to change his or her ways. A religious community and the state work together in this context to ensure that the religious convictions are upheld, on the one hand, and the rule of law is protected, on the other hand, because the Constitution is the supreme law of the land. Furthermore, the Christian community also instils good conduct and good manners on children who must be taught to have discipline and respect for elders, and this is done in most cases by punishing the children when

309. Section 10 of the Constitution.
310. Schoeman, *supra* n. 301, at 5.
311. Holy Bible Exodus Ch 31: Verse 18.

they defy the Christian laws or values that are communicated in the Bible.[312] This practice or value of punishment through corporal punishment used to be the way of also maintaining discipline and order in schools; however, the laws have since changed to such an extent that corporal punishment is considered a crime in South Africa today.[313]

148. Meaning both the state and the Christian community and other religious communities are no longer singing from the same hymnbook when it comes to the topic of corporal punishment. A teacher or parent in South Africa today cannot effect corporal punishment on a child without being dismissed or suspended from employment as a teacher or arrested or warned as a parent in some cases.[314] This is attributed to the fact that currently in South Africa corporal punishment is abolished and considered a crime and teachers and parents are encouraged to adopt other disciplinary measures to punish their children other than to go for corporal punishment, in order to avoid being in trouble with the law.

149. The values and principles of the Christian community is without a doubt similar to the other religious communities because the fundamental value that is key in all religious affiliations and communities is honesty and respect. This is key in relation to how people in the religious community relate with each other and other people, and it is important to note that religious communities are independent and autonomous on the basis of the trust and confidence they share with their members as already outlined. However, the autonomy and independence of religious communities is to a lesser or greater extent limited because it is still bound by the laws and procedures of the state and cannot encourage their members to engage in practices that are illegal and unlawful because this will be contrary to the public interest and unlawful. Religious communities are statutorily bound to ensure that in realising their mission and objectives they promote the interests and position of the state. This is attributed to the fact that a religious community occupies a strategic position of trust with its members, and this relationship cannot be underestimated at all by the state. Focus will now shift to the cultural community in South Africa that is subject to customary law and how it operates in the new democratic dispensation where human rights are upheld and protected.

II. Cultural Community under African Customary Law in New Democratic South Africa

150. The painful past of South Africa during the apartheid and colonial era has left a devastating effect on the application and development of cultural communities who are governed by African customary law. This was because African customary law was viewed as inferior to the common law and this resulted in cultural communities to be seen as non-existent or irrelevant because the legal system that

312. *Ibid.*
313. Section 10 of the South African Schools Act 1996.
314. *Ibid.*

governed them was not recognised.[315] This left most, if not all, of the various cultural communities in South Africa under-developed and poor, which is currently the *status quo* in the rural parts or provinces of South Africa post the democratic dispensation in South Africa.[316]

151. The democratic government with the adoption of the Constitution as the supreme law of the land had a duty to remedy the injustices of the past, which is to ensure that African customary law is developed and applied, to such an extent that it is put on the same level with the common law. This meant that African customary law must apply in parallel with the common law and does not need the common law to validate it, which was the position during the colonial and apartheid era period. Now only the Constitution can validate and confirm this legal system. The aim was to ensure that cultural communities are also protected and are independent through the application of a recognised legal system, which in this case is African customary law. Cultural communities are under the rule and governance of traditional leaders, who assume the role on the basis of birth, and in the past only male children could assume this role; however, this position has since changed because it was found to be discriminating against women on the basis of gender. This means that today a woman can be a leader of a traditional community in South Africa with the aim of ensuring peace and stability in that particular society.[317] It is believed that since traditional leadership is acquired by birth, a traditional leader is the one who shares some links or connection with ancestors for the development and prosperity of that cultural community. This link or connection with the ancestors makes the traditional leader a spiritual leader of the community.[318]

152. The traditional leader runs the traditional community in consultation with the traditional council, which is normally a group of elders who play the role of advisor and counsellor for the traditional leader. This is to safeguard the traditional leader from engaging in arbitrary decisions, which can harm the community.[319] Cultural communities are governed by African customary law, which also outlines the roles and powers of a traditional leader in the community because the interest of all the members of the community are key rather than individual interests.[320] The role and functions of a traditional leader in a cultural community is to provide support and care to members of the community; to allocate land to members of the community for residential and agricultural purposes; to provide safety in case of war; to provide or mete out the administration of justice through indigenous courts in case there is a dispute between members of the community and to ultimately ensure that there is peace and stability in the entire community.[321] The traditional leader will be executing all these functions under African customary law, and the traditional leader will ensure that discipline and order are achieved to such an extent that corporal

315. Mndende, *supra* n. 84, at 23.
316. *Ibid.*, at 24.
317. Bekker & Rautenbach, *supra* n. 18, at 48.
318. *Ibid.*
319. *Ibid.*, at 199.
320. *Ibid.*
321. *Ibid.*, at 200.

punishment and fines can be imposed in cases where a crime is committed, such as stock theft or a delict like adultery.[322] However, if a traditional leader engages on corporal punishment to such an extent that the wrong doer is injured, it will mean that such a traditional leader must be charged with assault and imprisoned on the basis that corporal punishment has been abolished in South Africa.[323] A similar case was reported in 2015 of *S v. Dalindyebo* in which the Pondo king was engaged in activities of assault, attempted murder and arson in meting out punishment to one of his subjects and was sentenced to twelve years of imprisonment for such illegal acts.[324] This court case and the assertions raised above do confirm that even though a cultural community is recognised in South Africa, and operating under African customary law is not without a doubt an independent community that operates parallel with the state, such a cultural community is subject to the Constitution and the rule of law.

153. The legal subjects or people that belong to a cultural community are bound by the authority of the traditional leader who can be either a king or a queen, depending on the clan and the circumstances of each clan or cultural community. The customs and traditions of that particular community will govern their daily lives and activities, which will promote their way of life and well-being. The customs and traditions of a cultural community will include encouraging group interests rather than individual needs on the basis that the needs of a group build a community for the betterment of tomorrow.[325] Respect and tolerance for elders and other people in general, which is key for the well-being of a particular individual and the broader community, is fundamental and encouraged. This goes with the aspect on the observance and recognition of cultural practices such as appeasing the ancestors and praying for rain among other things.[326] Dressing in indigenous clothes like lion skin among other things for men, and to engage in lawful customary marriages which can be either monogamous or polygamous in nature with the aim of procreation in a lawful and honourable manner to ensure that growth and sustainability in a cultural community are endorsed.[327] One of the distinguishing features of cultural communities in South Africa apart from other communities is the principle of restorative justice. This means that members of the community who are in dispute with each other will have to negotiate and speak with each other to resolve their disputes in an amicable manner. The traditional leader who will play a vital role in resolving the dispute of the parties will champion the same approach because no retribution or prisons are condoned or permitted in cultural communities.[328]

154. Even though traditional communities find themselves under traditional rule and administration, they are autonomous and independent. However, these communities and the traditional leaders are assisted by the local government through the

322. *Ibid.*
323. Section 10 of the South African Schools Act.
324. *S v. Dalindyebo* (090/2015) [2015] ZASCA 144 (1 Oct. 2015).
325. Mndende, *supra* n. 84, at 24.
326. *Ibid.*, at 25.
327. *Ibid.*
328. Bekker & Rautenbach, *supra* n. 18, at 201.

various municipalities spread out in the country, with the aim of ensuring that service delivery, such as the provision of water and sanitation, is provided to the people.[329] This means that there is co-operation between traditional leaders and the state when it comes to the running of traditional communities, particularly in the area of service delivery and administration. This collaborative approach is something that has been exploited by both traditional leaders and the state because traditional leaders would edge and encourage members of their society to vote for a particular political party on the basis that it is working for the needs of the community. In return, the political party that has been voted in power can return the favour through the provision of gifts and donations to the relevant traditional leader and his or her community.[330] Furthermore, the relationship between traditional leaders and government has been strengthened today in South Africa because all traditional leaders receive some form of remuneration from the state on the basis of their position. This form of benefits and privileges make or put traditional leaders in a position where they are able to promote the interests of the state to all the members of their community because they are in a position of trust and power with their subjects in the community. A similar stance that was identified when discussing the position of a religious community above. The fact that a traditional community shares some links or benefits as provided by the Constitution does not mean that such a community can do as it pleases. It must ensure to promote the spirit, purpose and objective of the Bill of Rights in South Africa, meaning that the rule of law must be upheld and protected at all costs. For instance, traditional leaders who promote or engage in illegal activities by violating the rights of people in their communities under the pretence of culture will be prosecuted by the state. This was the case where traditional leaders are seen as oppressing and discriminating against women based on gender or in cases where the children are abused by making them to be married to old men. This is based on forced marriages; these practices are contrary to human rights and not in line with the provisions of the Constitution.[331]

155. Traditional communities are also connected with each other and other communities through the principle of *Ubuntu,* which is embedded in all traditional communities, irrespective of the clan or language a person comes from or speaks. In all indigenous communities the values of respect, honesty, sharing, caring, love, compassion and solidarity are key. This is attributed to the fact that focus on a group and not an individual is championed, and it is important when it comes to traditional communities on the basis that a group is the one that makes and develops a community rather than a single individual who must become part of a group. For example, the principle of sharing and group emphasis in a traditional community is found where the eldest member of a family is working and the other members are unemployed. The eldest member of the family will ensure that he or she shares his or her salary with the rest of the members of the family with the aim of empowering those who are unemployed.[332] Meaning, that the interests of the member of

329. Section 150 of the Constitution.
330. Section 151 of the Constitution.
331. Section 2 of the Constitution.
332. Bekker & Rautenbach, *supra* n. 18, at 201.

the family, in this case as the eldest that works, are not taken into account, rather the interests of the entire family members for the purposes of their survival and development for the continued existence of the family and the community in turn.[333] Group interests are affirmed rather than the individual interests, which are in most instances seen to be selfish and not a way of life when it comes to a traditional community. In this, it is without a doubt affirmed that sharing is caring, and it is practiced on a daily basis in traditional communities.

§4. CONCLUSION

156. South Africa recognises religious and traditional communities based on their religion or cultural affiliations. These religious and traditional communities are autonomous and independent, but their independence and autonomy are subject to the rule of law and the Constitution as the supreme law. Religious and cultural communities cannot do or say something that is contrary to the Constitution or which will violate human rights and even to put the state in danger. The next chapter will focus on the fundamental rights, which religious communities enjoy in South Africa as protected by the Constitution.

333. *Ibid.*, at 202.

Chapter 2. Fundamental Rights and Religious Communities

§1. Introduction

157. Since religious and cultural communities are part of the population and state of South Africa, it means that these religious and cultural communities are under the supremacy and rule of the Constitution. Religious and cultural communities are entitled to the various fundamental rights, which are enshrined and protected by the Constitution, in addition to the various rights and responsibilities that emanate from that particular religious or cultural community.

158. The provision of fundamental rights by the state to members of the religious and cultural communities emanates from the responsibility the state owes to the citizens of South Africa with the aim of ensuring that they lead a productive and dignified life. Furthermore, the state has an obligation in ensuring that it realises these rights based on the reasonable available resources at its disposal. Various fundamental rights are provided by the Constitution in chapter two, which is the Bill of Rights, and a discussion about these rights as well as the application and limitation of the fundamental rights that are protected in the Bill of Rights will be explored. From the above assessment, it is clear that religious and cultural communities enjoy fundamental rights like any other citizen of the Republic, and this is because a person who is part of a religious or cultural community does not cease to be a citizen of the Republic of South Africa by voluntarily being part of a religious or cultural community.

§2. Chapter Two of the Bill of Rights of the Constitution of the Republic of South Africa, 1996

159. The Bill of Rights is found in chapter two of the Constitution and section 7(1) of the Constitution states that the Bill of Rights is the cornerstone of democracy in South Africa. It enshrines the rights of all people in our country and affirms the democratic values of human dignity, equality and freedom.[334] Section 7(2) of the Constitution provides for the realisation of the rights contained in the Bill of Rights by providing that the state must respect, protect, promote and fulfil the rights in the Bill of Rights.[335] Furthermore, section 7(3) of the Constitution states that the rights in the Bill of Rights are subject to the limitation clause as stated in section 36(1) or elsewhere in the Bill of Rights.[336] The question that now arises is who does the Bill of Rights apply to, or to put it differently, the question should be who is bound by the provisions of the Bill of Rights as it enshrines fundamental rights to all the people of South Africa, irrespective of their origin, colour, religion and culture.

---

334. Section 7(1) of the Constitution.
335. Section 7(2) of the Constitution.
336. Section 7(3) of the Constitution.

160. Section 8(1) of the Constitution states that the Bill of Rights applies to all law and binds the legislature, executive, judiciary and all organs of state.[337] Furthermore, section 8(2) of the Constitution provides that a provision in the Bill of Rights binds a natural or a juristic person if and to the extent that it is applicable, taking into account the nature of the right and the nature of any duty imposed by that right.[338] For the application and implementation of the fundamental rights that are contained in the Bill of Rights, section 8(3) of the Constitution states that when applying a provision of a Bill of Rights to a natural or juristic person in terms of subsection (2), a court: (a) in order to give effect to a right in the Bill of Rights must apply, or if necessary develop, the common law to the extent that legislation does not give effect to that right; and (b) may develop rules of common law to limit the right, provided that the limitation is in accordance with section 36(1).[339] Lastly, when it comes to the application of the rights contained in the Bill of Rights, section 8(4) of the Constitution states that a juristic person is entitled to the rights in the Bill of Rights to the extent required by the nature of the rights and the nature of that juristic person.[340] It is important to note that the Bill of Rights makes provision to a number of fundamental rights, which cannot be discussed in detail for this study. Apart from the fundamental right, which is the right to freedom to choose religion or culture on the part of an individual or group as already discussed, the discussion here will be limited to the central and core fundamental right, which is close to the hearts of all the people of South Africa, irrespective of their religion, culture, colour or creed, and it is the right to access healthcare services. The reason for limiting the discussion to only the right to access healthcare services is because it is one of the precious and safeguarded rights due to its importance in preserving and maintaining life. It is dear to both religious and cultural communities in South Africa, despite the fact that religious and cultural communities do hold the view that life is given by God and he alone can preserve and take it. This point is not disputed at all and the discussion on the right to access healthcare must be seen as a way the government relates with both religious and cultural communities in fulfilling fundamental rights.

161. Section 27(1) of the Constitution guarantees everyone the right to access healthcare services, which include reproductive healthcare, and that no one may be refused emergency medical treatment.[341] The government has a duty to fulfil this obligation to provide healthcare services to the people based on reasonable availability of resources, including the private healthcare sector, to a greater or lesser extent, particularly in emergency medical treatment.[342] This means that if healthcare practitioners deny people medical treatment or emergency medical treatment, their actions would amount to a violation of the right to access healthcare as protected by the Constitution.

---

337. Section 8(1) of the Constitution.
338. Section 8(2) of the Constitution.
339. Section 8(3) of the Constitution.
340. Section 8(4) of the Constitution.
341. Section 27(1) of the Constitution.
342. Section 27(2) of the Constitution.

162. Violating the protection of socio-economic rights, enshrined in the Constitution, goes against the purpose for which these rights were designed because chapter two of the Constitution is aimed at addressing the imbalances and injustices of the past. Further, to unfairly and unjustifiably deny or violate socio-economic rights constitutes a contravention of section 7(2) of the Constitution, which states that the government must respect, promote, protect and fulfil the rights in the Bill of Rights.[343] This provision clearly outlines the duty of government not only to refrain from interfering with the enjoyment of these rights, but also to promote, protect and enhance their realisation as part of its constitutional mandate.

163. The debate as to whether socio-economic rights are justiciable or not has long been settled in the South African context, evident from landmark court judgments, such as *Soobramoney v. Minister of Health (KwaZulu-Natal).*[344] This case will be discussed later in this chapter.

164. In this chapter, the focus will not be on the justifiability of socio-economic rights, but rather on the role of the courts in protecting socio-economic rights such as the right to access healthcare services. Brand argues that socio-economic rights can be enforced by the courts in two ways: first, through their lawmaking powers of interpreting legislation and developing the rules of common law, and second, the courts ought to adjudicate constitutional and other challenges experienced in state procedures that are intended to advance socio-economic rights.[345] The interpretation stated by Brand on the role of the courts in enforcing socio-economic rights is in line with sections 8(2)–8(3) of the Constitution, when it relates to the application and enforcement of the rights in the Bill of Rights.[346]

165. Treatment Action Campaign v. The Minister of Health[347] serves as a fundamental and instrumental case to the provision of section 27 of the Constitution. In this case, the applicants sought an order against the Minister of Health and the healthcare authorities of all nine provinces, except the Western Cape. The order requested was to compel the Minister and all healthcare authorities in the eight provinces to implement an effective national programme to prevent or reduce mother-to-child transmission of the HIV and Acquired Immune Deficiency Syndrome (AIDS) virus, which would include the dispensing of Nevirapine to pregnant women who are HIV positive, and to their babies. Nevirapine is described as an antiretroviral drug that can prevent or inhibit the spread of HIV.[348] The applicants in this case described to the court the alarming rate of mother-to-child transmission and the impressive reduction that would be achieved by the administration of the

343. Section 7(2) of the Constitution and *See* B. Bekink, *Principles of South African Constitutional Law* 81 (LexisNexis, Johannesburg 2012).
344. *Soobramoney v. Minister of Health, Kwazulu Natal* 1998 (1) SA 765 (CC).
345. D. Brand *Introduction to Socio-Economic Rights in the South African Constitution in Brand D and Heyns C Socio-Economic Rights in South Africa* 1 (Butterworths, Durban 2005).
346. Section 8(2) of the Constitution.
347. *Treatment Action Campaign (TAC) v. The Minister of Health* 2002 (4) BCLR 356 (T).
348. *Ibid.*, at 357.

drug.[349] It was claimed in court that a single dose of the drug can reduce this form of transmission by 50%, but this claim was disputed by the respondents who maintained that the success rate was probably considerably lower.[350] The respondents further in general contended that immediate implementation of antiretroviral treatment in these cases would be impossible because of insufficient financial resources.[351]

166. Judge Botha concluded, with regard to section 27 of the Constitution, that a countrywide prevention programme of this kind is an ineluctable obligation of the state.[352] Moreover, Nevirapine would be affordable if the programme is properly planned. What was required in the opinion of the court was a plan striving towards a comprehensive coverage and implementation of Nevirapine. The court accordingly made an order to this effect.[353] The court also made it clear that to order an immediate roll-out of the drug would be impossible and not practical, and as a result of this view, it ordered the respondents to report back to it within three months regarding the status of planning for the implementation of the roll-out of the drug. In this case, the court ruled in favour of the applicants.[354]

167. This decision of the high court was confirmed by the Constitutional Court,[355] as it reasoned that government policy, which provides for the availability of the Nevirapine drug in only certain areas of public hospitals, was inflexible and unconstitutional. Government was ordered to roll-out the administration of Nevirapine nationally for preventing mother-to-child transmission of HIV.[356]

168. Furthermore, section 27(2) of the Constitution provides that government must take legislative and other measures within its reasonable resources to achieve the progressive realisation of each of these rights.[357] What constitutes 'reasonable resources' will be determined on the basis of the facts of each case. Despite the fact that the right to access healthcare services is constitutionally enshrined, it is still important to note that considerable inequalities exist with regard to access to healthcare services. These inequalities are largely caused by the discrepancies found in healthcare resources and barriers to access health, such as vast distances, high travelling costs from rural areas, long queues and disempowered patients. As already discussed colonial past had a negative effect on the rural landscapes of South Africa not only from a religious and cultural point of view but also from an access to healthcare perspective.[358] For example, in *Soobramoney v. Minister of Health*

349. *Ibid.*
350. *Ibid.*, at 358.
351. *Ibid.*, at 360.
352. *Ibid.*, at 361.
353. *Ibid.*, at 362.
354. *Ibid.*, at 364.
355. *Ibid.*, at 365.
356. *Ibid.*
357. Section 27(2) of the Constitution.
358. M. Chersich, *Inequalities in Access to Health Care in South Africa*, 32 JPHP 3 (2011).

(KwaZulu-Natal),[359] the court dealt with the issue of unavailability of healthcare services to a patient who was suffering from kidney failure, but had been denied treatment in the relevant public hospital. The conduct of the hospital was found to be justified due to the lack of resources and in line with the provisions of the Constitution.[360]

§3. Public and Private Healthcare in South Africa

169. In South Africa, similar to most developing countries, the provision of healthcare services is divided into two sectors, namely the private healthcare sector and the public healthcare sector. In South Africa, these two systems of healthcare treatment were established during the apartheid era and are still sustained in the modern-day democratic South Africa.[361] In order to contextualise the two systems of healthcare, it is necessary to provide a brief history relating to how these two systems of healthcare were formed during the apartheid era. During apartheid, the quality and nature of healthcare services were based on three factors, namely race, location and income.[362] Homelands were formed with the aim of formally separating people in different areas, and thus the same principle was applied to healthcare services, which were inadequately and poorly administered to the majority of black people in the homelands.[363]

170. During apartheid, the church played a significant role in the administration of healthcare services to the majority of the people, due to the failure of the then government in providing healthcare services to the people in the public sector setting.[364] This shows that religion did not only play a major role in the political struggle of South Africa but went beyond in such a way that healthcare services were provided by religious groups at some point in South Africa. The formation of the private sector came into existence as a result of the economic downturn and the pressure which was placed on the government by the medical industry, resulting in the government having to regulate the healthcare sector.[365] Through the regulation of the healthcare sector, the private healthcare sector rose as an institution of healthcare services. How healthcare is administered in both the private and public sectors will be discussed now.

---

359. *Soobramoney v. Minister of Health, supra* n. 345, at 765.
360. *Ibid.*, at 766.
361. S. Beck, *Health Policy, Health Services, and Cancer Pain Management in the New South Africa*, 17 JPSM 17 (1999).
362. D. McIntyre, *The Health and Health System of South Africa: Historical Roots of Current Public Health Challenges*, 374 Lancet 817 (2009).
363. S.M. Tollman & K. Kautzky, *A Perspective on Primary Health Care in South Africa* 2 SAHR 20 (2008).
364. *Ibid.*, at 21.
365. C.D. Naylor *Private Medicine and the Privatization of Health Care in South Africa* 11 Social Science & Medicine 1153 (1998).

I. Private Healthcare Services

171. It is estimated that only 15% of the South African population has access to private hospital treatment.[366] In private hospitals, for example, cancer and other health-related treatments are found to be effective and functional.[367]Such efficiency and effectiveness are achieved by means of readily available drugs and the presence of state of the art medical equipment.[368] Private healthcare system is accessed by those with access to insurance or medical aid funding, or those who can afford to pay for it directly from their own pockets.[369] Private healthcare treatment, compared with the public healthcare treatment accounts for the largest share of total healthcare financing, which comprises of medical aid schemes and private out-of-pocket payments made by patients.[370] Private healthcare treatment is generally viewed as the best available, and it is seen to be the most effective with regard to cancer treatment and other chronic medical conditions.[371]

172. However, there are challenges with regard to private healthcare system, as it is generally expensive to access, and thus is not easily accessible to the indigent who mostly are part of the religious and cultural communities of South Africa who need the quality of care offered in private institutions.[372] As a consequence, some medical aid schemes are not willing to pay for cancer treatment and other chronic medical conditions in private institutions, due to the high cost associated with treatment in the private healthcare system. One example of this situation is the case of a woman who died in 2007 of breast cancer because her medical fund, Global Health, refused to pay for her treatment.[373]

---

366. *Ibid.*, at 1153.
367. *Ibid.*, 1154.
368. *Ibid.*
369. Chersich, *supra* n. 359, at 102.
370. J. Akazili & J. Ataguba, *Health Care Financing in South Africa: Moving Towards Universal Coverage*, 28 CEM 75 (2010).
371. *Ibid.*, at 76.
372. *Ibid.*, at 77.
373. *Ibid.*, at 78. The Competition Tribunal commented on the state of healthcare in South Africa, and how the private healthcare system has become a lucrative business. The provision of adequate healthcare to all the citizens of the country is clearly an important plank in the government's efforts to tackle poverty and inequality. High and middle income earning South Africans (and this would include a significant proportion of those in employment) receive healthcare through South Africa's sophisticated private healthcare system comprising the full gamut of general practitioners, specialists, hospitals and pharmacies. Private healthcare system is funded by an array of medical schemes serviced by the administration companies, data processing companies and managed care companies that are an integral part of South Africa's sophisticated 'first world' private healthcare system. However, majority of the population (and this includes a significant number of those in the lower reaches of formal employment) rely on the public healthcare system for meeting its needs. The reality, and possibly the only agreed certainty in the fraught debate surrounding the provision of healthcare in South Africa, is that the private healthcare system, and most notably, although not exclusively, the private hospital network, is characterised by significantly excess capacity while the public healthcare system is simultaneously resource-constrained and increasingly unable to cope with the demands which it faces. A major thrust of the government's efforts to improve healthcare provisioning is thus to utilise the excess capacity in the private healthcare system, to reduce the

173. Section 27 of the Constitution also binds private hospitals to provide medical treatment to patients during an emergency situation.[374] In addition, section 5 of the National Health Act supports the position that both private and public healthcare establishments cannot deny anyone emergency medical treatment.[375] Pieterse argues that the constitutional obligation placed on both private and public hospitals to provide emergency medical treatment is a direct and immediate entitlement.[376] The question as to what constitutes emergency treatment has been left open by the Constitution. This has had serious financial implications on private hospitals as they are obliged to render emergency medical treatment to people who cannot guarantee the necessary payment.[377] Since the question of what constitutes emergency medical treatment has been left open by the Constitution, it is assumed to be a question of fact, which will be decided on a case-by-case basis. However, in the landmark case of *Soobramoney v. Minister of Health (KwaZulu-Natal)*,[378] discussed in detail below, the court defined emergency medical treatment as a 'sudden catastrophe which calls for immediate attention'.[379] The broad and flexible nature of this definition is supported because it caters for all forms of healthcare emergencies without excluding the other.

174. Due to the seriousness of the obligation to provide emergency medical treatment, and the inconsistencies of some private hospitals in implementing and realising this socio-economic right to healthcare services, specific legislation was enacted, which deserves to be mentioned. Item 3(b) of the Schedule to the Promotion of Equality and Prevention of Unfair Discrimination Act 4 of 2000 reinforces the obligation imposed on private hospitals to render emergency treatment to a patient by prohibiting the discriminatory refusal of emergency treatment.[380] As a consequence, a person living with cancer in an emergency situation may be admitted to a private hospital to receive treatment, and unfortunately, that particular hospital will be permitted to bill the patient for the services which they have rendered without taking into account whether the patient can afford the bill or not.

175. The obligation of private hospitals to admit patients in emergency situations is further stressed by the Hospital Association of South Africa; this association has incorporated a draft code of ethics for private hospitals across the country.[381] In the draft code of ethics for private hospitals, emergency treatment is defined as

---

demands on the public healthcare system, to move a strata of those presently reliant on public healthcare system over to the private healthcare system.

374. Section 27 of the Constitution.

375. Section 5 of the National Health Act.

376. M. Pieterse, *Enforcing the Right Not to Be Refused Emergency Medical Treatment: Towards Appropriate Relief*, 18 Stellenbosch Law Review 75 (2007).

377. M. Pieterse, *Legislative and Executive Translation of the Right to Have Access to Health Care Services*, 10 Law Democracy and Development 243 (2010).

378. *Soobramoney v. Minister of Health*, *supra* n. 345, at 766.

379. *Ibid.*, at para. 36.

380. Item 3(b) of the Schedule to the Promotion of Equality and Prevention of Unfair Discrimination Act 4 of 2000.

381. Proposed Code of Ethics for Private Hospitals – Hospital Association of South Africa *Private Hospital Review 2008: Examination of Factors Impacting on Private Hospitals* 67 HASA 44 (2008).

'treatment that is necessary to stabilise an emergency medical condition'.[382] The code requires private healthcare establishments to render such treatment ethically without any form of discrimination and subject to reasonable compensation. This definition of emergency medical treatment as provided for by the Hospital Association of South Africa is in line with the definition that was provided by the court in the *Soobramoney* case, because both definitions cover all forms of medical emergencies.[383]

II. Public Healthcare Services

176. Public healthcare treatment in South Africa is administered to 75% of the population, which is largely located in urban and rural areas, including religious and cultural communities.[384] The public healthcare treatment of cancer and other related illnesses is characterised by inadequate treatment facilities, less or unavailable drugs, overcrowding of patients, unqualified staff and abuse of patients by staff.[385] The public healthcare treatment system is often seen as the exact opposite of private healthcare treatment in the country. For example, persons living with breast cancer have to wait for weeks before undergoing surgery in the Groote Schuur Hospital situated in Cape Town,[386] due to the unavailability of funds from the National Department of Health. Not enough staff is available and in addition to this, defective, as well as old equipment, is used to assist patients.[387] Currently, in Durban there has been a shortage of oncologists to an extent that one oncologist is responsible for thousands of cancer patients, resulting in poor healthcare afforded to persons living with cancer in need of urgent healthcare.[388] National Department of Health has admitted that there is a shortage of oncologists across the country, and this is surely a call for concern when it comes to the treatment of cancer and other chronic conditions in South Africa.[389] If this problem is not resolved as soon as possible it means that millions of persons living with cancer in South Africa, who rely on public healthcare system, will either lose their lives or will be denied access to healthcare due to a shortage of oncologists in the country. This will be contrary to the fundamental right to healthcare as enshrined in the Constitution. These obstacles, in addition to the physical pain that persons living with cancer experience, cause a lot of distress for them and their families, and are unfortunately beyond their control.[390] Furthermore, this lack of healthcare services leaves people with only one hope, which is prayer to God for a divine intervention.

---

382. Clause 1 of the Proposed Code of Ethics for Private Hospitals 67.
383. *Soobramoney v. Minister of Health, supra* n. 345, at para. 36.
384. Falkson G and Beck S *Prevalence and Management of Cancer Pain in South Africa* 94 Pain 76 (2001).
385. Chersich, *supra* n. 1 at 103.
386. Falkson and Beck, *supra* n. 1 at 76.
387. Falkson and Beck, *supra* n. 1 at 77.
388. *Ibid.*
389. Chersich, *supra* n. 1 at 104.
390. Patijn J *High Prevalence of Pain in Patients with Cancer in a Large Population-Based Study in the Netherlands* 132 Pain 312 (2007).

177. Proper measures need to be taken to avoid or prevent the government from disregarding the realisation of the right to access healthcare services for all South Africans. However, this has proven to be an impossible task in the case of cervical cancer, where the screening process has already perpetuated and reinforced inequality with regard to the availability of such facilities.[391] This is because cancer-screening facilities are available only to a select few in South Africa. For instance, women in rural areas who live far away from clinics are deprived of this service, while those located in cities and urban areas, situated closer to hospitals and clinics, will have better access to these healthcare services.

178. Around 3,800 women, who mostly rely on public healthcare treatment, die of cervical cancer every year in South Africa.[392] This is a high percentage, which points to a potential problem in the public healthcare system. The Cancer Association of South Africa has stressed the importance of making screening programmes widely available for women for purposes of early detection of any cancer in order to reduce the number of deaths caused by cancer.[393] Patients making use of public hospitals may compel the hospital to provide treatment to them, but this may be limited, as the state will provide the treatment based on its available resources in accordance with section 27 of the Constitution.

§4. *Soobramoney v. Minister of Health (Kwazulu-Natal)* 1998 (1) SA 765 (CC)

179. This case involved a patient who was in need of dialysis treatment on a weekly basis, as he was suffering from kidney failure and needed treatment in order to survive.[394] The state argued that there were not enough facilities to offer this treatment as it was expensive.[395] The state, however, would provide treatment based on available resources in order to preserve the life of the patient in question.[396] The court further reasoned that the decision of the Minister of Health was made in good faith and through rational decision-making, found to be in the best interest of the public, and therefore did not warrant any interference by the court.[397] The court ruled in favour of the Minister and refused to compel the hospital to act in the manner that the patient anticipated, but it confirmed that the decision of the hospital in question was based on its available resources in its provision of treatment, and as expected according to section 27 of the Constitution.[398]

---

391. Denny L, Kuhn L and Batra P *Utilisation and Outcomes of Cervical Cancer Prevention Services Among HIV-Infected Women in Cape Town* 100 SAMJ 39 (2010).
392. Express C *More Services Needed to Fight Cancer* 23 UFS 8 (2008).
393. *Ibid.*, at 9.
394. *Soobramoney v. Minister of Health, supra* n. 345, at 1697.
395. *Ibid.*
396. *Soobramoney v. Minister of Health, supra* n. 345, at 1698.
397. *Soobramoney v. Minister of Health, supra* n. 345, at 1699.
398. *Ibid.* In *Government of Republic of South Africa and others v. Grootboom*, (CCT11/00) [2000] ZACC 19; 2001 (1) SA 46; 2000 (11) BCLR 1169 (4 Oct. 2000), the facts involve the eviction of informal residents of a privately owned land which was reserved for the construction of low-cost

180. Based on the provision of section 27(2) of the Constitution and the *Soobramoney* case, one can deduce that the right to access healthcare services, as guaranteed in section 27(1) of the Constitution, is not absolute, in the sense that it is dependent on the availability of reasonable resources.[399] As to what really constitutes reasonable resources surely needs a precise definition. The vagueness of reasonableness in this context entails that a patient's fate in a public healthcare establishment would depend on the available resources, without the hospital being held liable for a lack thereof. The public healthcare establishment may argue that it acted within the limits of its reasonable resources to save the life of the patient. The issue of reasonable resources in the provision of healthcare services is a form of a qualified step to the provision of healthcare services, requiring closer investigation as to what it entails, and the effect it has on the overall right to healthcare services as provided for in the Constitution.

181. The first step in addressing the vagueness of the concept of reasonable resources as stated in section 27 of the Constitution is to accept the position that was followed in *Government of Republic of South Africa and others v. Grootboom.*[400] In this case, the standard of reasonableness was adopted to test the relevant legislation regarding its fulfilment or realisation of socio-economic rights. The case is relevant for this discussion since the right to have access to healthcare services is also a socio-economic right and forms the point of discussion at present. According to the court, any measures which are adopted with the aim of fulfilling socio-economic rights ought to encompass a standard that is reasonable in both its conceptualisation and implementation.[401] This simply means that there must be a clear allocation of tasks and responsibilities to different stakeholders in government, and appropriate financial and human resources must be made available in order to realise socio-economic rights. This reasoning of the court regarding the duty of government to fulfil socio-economic rights is in line with the International Covenant on Economic, Social and Cultural Rights (ICESCR), of which South Africa is a member.[402] This international human rights instrument states that in order for a state party to be able to attribute its failure to meet at least its minimum

---

houses. The residents opposed their eviction by the government on the basis that the government was obliged to provide them with alternative or temporary shelter as enshrined by the Constitution, until they acquired permanent accommodation with their offsprings. The court held that the government was obliged to provide temporary or alternative shelter, on demand, to children and parents and in instances where parents are unable to accommodate their own children. The court further reasoned that this duty by the government to provide shelter to the people is independent and the state must take reasonable legislative and other measures within its disposal to realise this goal. In this case the court concluded by outlining that the state was obliged to provide temporary accommodation to the evicted dwellers without taking into account the aspect of availability of resources; this was due to the fact that there was a crisis and an emergency. The appeal court, however, was in disagreement with the court of *a quo* when it came to this decision. *Government of the Republic of SA v. Grootboom*, *ibid.*, at 1169.

399. Section 36(1) of the Constitution.
400. *Government of the Republic of SA v. Grootboom, supra* n. 399, at 1169.
401. *Ibid.*
402. ICESCR Adopted and opened for signature, ratification and accession by General Assembly Resolution 2200 A (XXI) of 16 Dec. 1966 and came into force on 3 Jan. 1976 in accordance with Article 27 of the UN.

core obligations to a lack of resources, it must demonstrate that every effort was made to use all resources that are at its disposition to satisfy, as a matter of priority, those minimum obligations.

182. The most important aspect which the court highlighted in the *Soobramoney* case is that legislation or policy which is aimed at the realisation of socio-economic rights must be transparent and communicated effectively to all the parties concerned, in order for it to be effectively implemented without confusion. However, this is unfortunately the current state of affairs particularly in South Africa's public healthcare system.[403] Pieterse argues that the non-fulfilment of the right to access healthcare services for patients in public healthcare system is not only attributed to inadequate legislation and healthcare policy, but it is also due to failures to translate and interpret the right to its correct meaning and aim.[404] Pieterse's view is correct, as this problem has arisen in the context of determining what constitutes reasonable resources as provided for in section 27(2) of the Constitution.[405]

183. The major challenge in both private and public hospitals in South Africa is the shortage of qualified staff. This challenge results in a frustration of the relationships between patients and medical personnel.[406] In the context of cancer and other chronic medical conditions, the shortage of staff will result in the unavailability of necessary resources and support to deal with the demands of the oncology unit.[407] The problem of shortage of staff is not only a challenge in South Africa, between the private and public healthcare centres, but affects the entire African continent, and it has become a major factor in crippling healthcare systems on the continent.[408]

184. In Africa, 10,000 medical professionals graduate each year, but within five years, about half of them leave for Europe in search of greener pastures.[409] Most African graduates leave their countries due to low salaries, restricted career development options and work overload, which is a common feature in the African healthcare systems.[410] Change is urgently required, which may be done by providing career counselling in medical schools and professional institutions, as well as the provision of mentorship programmes to students. Offering incentives to generate an interest and commitment among young medical professionals in order for them to stay in Africa and not go abroad is also a mechanism that may possibly alleviate the problem.[411]

403. *Government of the Republic of SA v. Grootboom*, *supra* n. 399, at 1170.
404. Pieterse, *supra* n. 378, at 251.
405. *Ibid.*, at 252.
406. M. Venter, C. Venter & K. Botha, *Cancer Treatment in South Africa: A Narrative Literature Review* 22 JPA 462 (2012).
407. *Ibid.*, at 463.
408. *Ibid.*
409. I.F. Adewole, *Challenges and Opportunities in Cancer Control in Africa: A Perspective from the African Organisation for Research and Training in Cancer* 14 Series 147 (2013).
410. *Ibid.*.
411. *Ibid.*, at 148.

§5. Conclusion

185. From the above assessment, it is clear that members of a religious or cultural community too suffer from different chronic diseases like cancer, and they experience challenges in accessing healthcare services. Access to healthcare services as protected and enshrined in the Constitution is key to the survival of religious and cultural communities as well as the broader public of South Africa. This is despite believing in God or ancestors, the right to healthcare services as protected in the Constitution cannot be underestimated but must be championed and realised for the continued existence and health of the South African population. Furthermore, government must work hard to ensure that this right is realised and due to the current state of public healthcare system in South Africa, a collaboration between the private and public healthcare sectors is encouraged. This will be seen as the first step in addressing the challenges that are faced by the public healthcare sector, and it will be an opportunity for the private and public healthcare sectors to learn from each other. The aim in this learning experience will be to enhance the healthcare system of South Africa, which without a doubt will be in the public interests.

Chapter 3. Contractual Religious Freedom

§1. Introduction

186. The practice and freedom of religion or culture is a voluntary process in the sense that the individual is the one that chooses to follow or to subscribe to a particular religion or culture on their own volition. This means that one cannot be pushed or forced to take part in a particular religion or culture against their will in South Africa because this will be viewed as contrary to the freedom to choose a religion or culture of one's choice as expressly guaranteed and protected by the Constitution.

187. Since the practice and participation of religion and culture is a voluntary process, which the individual person expresses to a particular religion or culture, the question that now arises is whether or not a contract exists between the religious freedom of an individual and a particular religion or culture? If there is such a contract, then it is considered as the horizontal application of rights or an equal relationship as per the Constitution. Furthermore, it can be asked if there is a relationship between a religious or cultural society and the state, it can be classified as the vertical application of rights and is normally an unequal relationship between the state and its citizens. The aim of this chapter will be to explore the relationship between an individual and a religious society and to further explore the relationship between a religious community and the state in line with the Constitution as the supreme law of the land.

§2. Individual and Collective Contractual Religious or Cultural Freedom

188. An individual and the collective, which normally is a group or community, enjoy the freedom to choose their own religious or cultural beliefs as protected by the Constitution.[412] However, does this freedom to choose religion or cultural beliefs on the part of an individual or collective amount to a contract with that religion or cultural belief, and the answer to this question is yes on the following basis. The fact that religious and cultural beliefs are entered into voluntarily without any pressure on the part of an individual or collective creates a form of a contract between the religious or cultural belief and the particular individual or group. For example, a person who chooses to subscribe to a certain religious and cultural belief also agrees to the personal laws that come with those religious or cultural beliefs.[413] This means that an individual or the group take the responsibility to uphold and protect the personal laws or codes which stem from that particular religion or cultural

412. Section 15 of the Constitution.
413. *Personal Law,* https://www.merriam-webster.com/dictionary/personal%20law (accessed 11 Jun. 2018).

belief while at the same time the religious or cultural organisation aims to uplift and make the individual or group to grow spiritually and to uphold their human dignity in the process.[414]

189. One can say that the relationship or contract that exists between a religious or cultural belief with an individual or group is reciprocal in nature and this emanates from the fact that the individual or group is bound to uphold the dignity and reputation of that religious or cultural belief. In turn, the religious or cultural belief has the responsibility to not discriminate or violate the rights of an individual or group as their members.[415] This means that, for example, a religious or cultural belief which an individual or group has chosen voluntary cannot discriminate that individual on the basis that he is gay, as this type of conduct by either the religious or cultural belief will be contrary to public policy, and it will be in breach of contract between the individual concerned and that religious or cultural belief.[416] In South Africa it is important to mention that there has been lots of disputes which are in connection with the discrimination of congregants who are either gay or lesbian and who have been excluded by the church on the basis of their sexual orientation. This conduct by the various churches was found to be discriminatory and in breach of contractual religious freedom between an individual and the church and in most cases the church was called on to correct and stop engaging in practices that are discriminatory and contrary to the provisions of the Constitution as the supreme law of the land.[417] The same can be said about an individual or group that belongs to a religious or cultural belief and engages in conduct that tarnish or put the religious or cultural belief into disrepute. In this case the conduct of either the individual or collective will be discouraged and in some instances the individual or group concerned will be put through disciplinary proceedings with the aim of restoring the integrity of that particular religious or cultural belief.[418]

190. The relationship between an individual and a group with a religious or cultural affiliation is based on a horizontal application as provided by section 8(1) of the Constitution.[419] This type of relationship is equal between the parties and the same can be said with the contractual relationship between an individual and a religious or cultural affiliation in terms of exercising the freedom to religion and culture. An individual can hold a religious or cultural affiliation accountable for acting contrary to the law and *vice versa*, in cases where the terms of their contractual freedom to religion or culture are not upheld but violated. By outlining that this is an equal relationship it means that both an individual and a religious or cultural affiliation are on equal footing, and no one exercises more power on the other but are equal in the exercise of their role and function in realising this contractual freedom to religion as enshrined and protected by the Constitution.

---

414. Section 10 of the Constitution.
415. Section 9 of the Constitution.
416. Section 9(1) of the Constitution.
417. *Ibid.*
418. *Personal Law*, https://www.merriam-webster.com/dictionary/personal%20law (accessed 12 Jun. 2018).
419. Section 8(1) of the Constitution.

191. Voluntariness lies at the heart of the contract between the religious or cultural affiliation and the individual or group. This in the sense means that in realising the contractual freedom to religion or culture the state cannot compel its citizens to follow a certain religion or culture because this will be contrary to the requirements for a valid religious or cultural freedom as provided by the Constitution.[420] Furthermore, this implies that the state must embrace diversity and the various religious and cultural practices in South Africa without interfering or prescribing the type of religion or culture the people must follow. It must be left to an individual or group to exercise their right. Where it is found that the state has entered into a space of pushing people to a certain religion or culture at the exclusion of other religions or culture, such conduct will be a violation of contractual freedom to religion and a violation of the right to freedom to choose religion or culture freely as protected by the Constitution.[421]

192. The same applies to parents. They cannot compel their children to follow a certain religion or culture, but they can play a role in ensuring that their children grow up in a particular religion or culture. This does not mean that the children are bound to follow the religion or culture in which they grew up, or be compelled to follow it once they are old. Children once they reach the age of majority, which is 18 years in South Africa, they are considered to be old and have the liberty to choose the religion or culture they would want to be associated with.[422] As long as that particular child is now a major and there is no other factor that serves as a deterrence towards affecting the mental capacity of that child, then such a child is also entitled to voluntarily choose his or her own religion or culture without the interference of parents or community.[423] In turn, the child is expected to abide by the rules or procedures of that particular religion or culture he or she has chosen, without undue influence or pressure. Mental illness, intoxication and provocation are some of the factors which are used to determine the capacity or state of mind of an individual and to measure if a person is able to draw a distinction between right and wrong.[424] These factors will aid when determining the voluntariness of a person to subscribe to a particular religion or culture.

193. Schools and workplaces are also duty bound to respect the voluntary aspect of an individual in relation to contractual freedom to religion or culture. Meaning a school or workplace cannot compel a student or an employee to subscribe to a particular culture or religion that is dominating in that particular school or workplace. Space must be provided for diversity and tolerance in the workplace or school with the aim of ensuring that the contractual religious freedom which an individual has chosen is not violated as protected by the Constitution.[425] Reasonable accommodation is one of the factors that needs to be adopted in the workplace and schools with the purpose of ensuring that diversity and tolerance are embraced in such a way that

420. Section 15(1) of the Constitution.
421. *Ibid.*
422. Section 12 Children's Act.
423. Section 12(1) Children's Act.
424. Section 14 Children's Act.
425. Section 15(1) of the Constitution.

no religious or cultural practice is discriminated against or undermined irrespective of its popularity and dominance in South Africa.[426] The principle of reasonable accommodation is more of a labour law concept and its meaning, purpose and value in the South African labour context will be explored extensively later on when discussing whether ministers qualify as employees in South Africa.

§3. The Relationship Between the State and Religious or Cultural Affiliations in Realising Contractual Freedom to Religion

194. The state has an important role to play in the relationship between religious or cultural affiliations and individuals or groups, despite the fact that such a relationship is private and voluntary in nature. Government's role in this relationship is based on the principle of the vertical application as provided by section 8(1) of the Constitution which is an unequal relationship.[427] This relationship is unequal on the basis that the state is the one that exercises more power on the individual and the individual is the one that must comply with the rules and procedures that have been set by the government in this regard.[428] An example of this form of relationship is the paying of taxes and an individual who defaults on paying taxes will be held liable for non-compliance, and it is a criminal offence not only in South Africa but across the globe.

195. In this unequal relationship the role of government is that of regulator and overseer, in how religious and cultural affiliations relate with their members. This means that the government ensures that people are not abused or degraded under the pretence of religion or culture because it has been proven on a number of occasions that culture and religion can be used to the detriment of people. The same can be said in South Africa in which the Commission for the Promotion and Protection of the Rights of Cultural, Religious and Linguistic Communities (CRL) has on a number of occasions exposed the inhumane and degrading practices of charismatic churches in South Africa, in which people are expected to eat grass and snakes, as part of religion.[429] Such practices are seen as contrary to human rights, such as the right to dignity among other things and pastors who were caught subjecting their congregants to these practices were arrested and prosecuted for violating the laws of the Republic.[430]

---

426. Section 15(1) of the Employment Equity Act 55 of 1998 deals with reasonable accommodation and encourages employers to embrace diversity in the workplace with the aim of protecting the rights of people, including the right to choose religion or culture.
427. Section 8(1) of the Constitution.
428. Section 8(2) of the Constitution.
429. Section 181 of the Constitution provides for the establishment of the CRL Commission which is a chapter nine institution and draws its mandate from the Constitution as the supreme law and this commission aims to safeguard the abuse of religious and cultural practices to the detriment of the people of South Africa.
430. Section 10 of the Constitution.

196. Currently, in South Africa as one of the measures to ensuring that religion and cultural practices are not abused which has been the case of late. The state through the CRL makes sure that churches and cultural institutions comply with the law. Furthermore, churches and cultural organisations are now expected to disclose their finances, church practices and culture with the aim of ensuring that the people of South Africa are not subjected to unnecessary abuse under the pretence of religion or culture which has unfortunately been the norm. The regulatory conduct of the state in this context is very much clear that it aims to uphold and protect the contractual freedom to religion which exists between an individual or a group and a particular religion or culture, while at the same time without any abuse being the order of the day.

197. Regulation on the part of the state does not take away the power or autonomy of an individual or group and the particular religion or culture, but it aims to ensure that the constitutional provision to freedom of religion is protected and preserved and that the rule of law is upheld all the time. This is attributed to the fact that the Constitution is the supreme law of the land and any law or conduct found to be contrary to the Constitution must be declared null and void.[431] However, the regulatory and supervisory role on the part of the state is not the only factor that is necessary for the preservation of the contractual freedom to religion or culture. The state has a working relationship with religious and cultural organisations by providing them with the necessary support and finances among other things. Furthermore, the state regards religious and cultural organisations as non-profit organisations and provide tax exemptions to these organisations in the interest of the public of South Africa and also to realise the freedom to religion or culture as protected.[432] In addition to these concessions by the state on religious and cultural organisations, these organisations are also duty bound to ensure that they comply with the rule of law and that they promote the government and the supremacy of the Constitution.

198. This means that the relationship between an individual and a particular religious or cultural group is reciprocal, and the same can be said about the relationship between the state and a religious or cultural organisation. For example, the state cannot prescribe the internal processes of a religious or cultural organisation, and a religious or cultural organisation cannot engage in conduct that put the state at risk or violates the human rights of its members, as this conduct will be contrary to the law and breach of the relationship of the two organisations.[433] The state and religious or cultural organisations work hand in glove with the aim of ensuring that the contractual freedom to religion an individual or group enjoys is realised and protected.

199. Since the state is also bound by the Constitution it ensures that it does not put in place policies or structures that serve as deterrence on people and religious or

431. Section 2 of the Constitution.
432. Section 21 of the Companies Act.
433. Section 8(1) of the Constitution.

cultural organisations to realise the contractual freedom to religion or culture. Government is duty bound to take its mandate from the Constitution and not exercise its powers in an arbitrary manner in its role of overseeing and regulating in this important relationship between an individual or group and a particular religion or culture. One can also argue that the overseeing role of government can be limited to a lesser or greater extent by section 36(1) of the Constitution, in cases where it is found that government is abusing its position.[434]

§4. CONCLUSION

200. In conclusion, from the observations above it is clear that the contractual freedom to religion or culture emanates from the principle of voluntariness. One must subscribe to a particular culture or religion freely without undue pressure or fear from anyone or the state for that matter. This chapter and the previous chapter were based on the domestic position of South African law, when it comes to the position and championing of the right to freedom of religion and culture. In the following chapters focus will shift to the international perspectives when it comes to religious law.

434. Section 36(1) of the Constitution.

Part IV. International, Transnational, Regional Effects on Religious Communities

Chapter 1. International Law Effects on Religious Communities

§1. Introduction

201. From the position of domestic law in the recognition of religious communities to the international perspective in the recognition and upliftment of religious communities in the international platform. Since the local position in South Africa has been explicitly outlined in terms of giving recognition to religious communities and they are regarded as independent communities, which enjoy autonomy from state intervention or interference in terms of their day-to-day operations and personal laws. However, as it was discussed, this independence is subject to the rule of law and the supremacy of the Constitution.

202. In this chapter, the focus will be on the role of international law in relation to the recognition of religious communities in ensuring that these religious communities are protected and preserved apart from the domestic laws that are in place as per each jurisdiction. Reference will be made to the relationship between international law and religion as a first point of departure and then the role of international law as well as international tribunals like the International Criminal Court (ICC) play in this particular sphere. Various court cases and also legal instruments on an international scale will be explored in this chapter, with the aim of highlighting the importance and role of international law towards religious communities.

§2. Relationship Between Religion and International Law

203. There is a close relationship between religion and international law because both of them aim to achieve social cohesion in different parts of the world. That is the reason why it can be argued in this case that religion has never been completely exiled from international law, but has always been part of international law venture.[435] Indeed, religion has played and continues to play a significant role in the

435. D. Evans, *Religion and International Law: Friends or Foes?*, 32 SOAS 638 (2010).

evolution of international law even though this relationship is often perceived to be complex and controversial for different reasons. On the one hand, the controversy surrounding this relationship may be attributed to the apparent differences in the nature of religion (sacred) and that of international law (secular).[436] Evans argues that the place of religion in the international legal system, or any legal system that purports to be secular, is likely to be controversial and complex.[437] On the other hand, religion and international law are identical in other ways. Generally, both religion and international law are important social phenomena that relate respectively to fundamental social issues in human society, which have often stimulated passionate disagreement about their proper content and functions.[438]

204. Both can be seen as systems of social ordering, as ethical or normative regimes or semi-autonomous social fields. Also, both religion and international law can be politicised and manipulated by elites, which adds further to the complexity of their relationship.[439] Owing to this complexity, the relationship between religion and international law can be analysed from different perspectives, depending on one's objective into the enquiry between religion and international law.[440] Based on the close relationship that exists between religion and international law, the question is whether religion and international law are friends or foes, and this question will be answered by the discussion of the various theories that aim to describe best the relationship that exists between religion and international law in ensuring that social cohesion is attained universally. One of the points that emerge is that there exists an old and ongoing relationship between religion and international law, which would be very difficult, if not impossible, to dissolve.[441] The strings of that romance are however in the hands of people, as human agents for both religion and international law, and they can be pulled for better or for worse.[442] This is where both a religious community and international law agencies need to pull together to ensure that social cohesion is maintained and preserved. Neither the separationist theory, which argues that religion and international law must be separated, nor the accomodationist theory, which is based on the idea that religion and international law must work together and if there is a conflict between the two then a compromise needs to be achieved, brings the best out of this relationship between religion and international law.[443] The strict adherence to the separationist theory portrays an adversarial relationship between religion and international law, or even promotes such a relationship and it closes the eyes of society to the positive contributions that religion has made, and could still make, to enhance and legitimise modern international law.[444]

436. *Ibid.*, at 638.
437. *Ibid.*, at 639.
438. *Ibid.*
439. *Ibid.*, at 640.
440. *Ibid.*
441. F.A. Boyle, *Foundations of World Order: The Legalistic Approach to International Relations 1898–1922* 1 (Duke University Press 1999).
442. *Ibid.*, at 2.
443. *Ibid.* .
444. *Ibid.*, at 3.

205. The accomodationist theory portrays a harmonistic picture between religion and international law, but its idealistic tendency may lead society too naively to disregard areas of tension which need careful consideration and resolution for the benefit of our common humanity.[445] This leads to the conclusion that the relationship between religion and international law should be objectively perceived as double-edged and capable of being either amicable or adversarial, depending on what society and human agents of the relationship between religion and international law want it to be. Meaning that the relationship between religion and international law is not always smooth sailing, but there are conflicts between the two systems and dialogue is key in ensuring that the said conflicts are resolved through a process of accommodation and negotiation among other things.

206. On the one hand, the importance of international law will continue to be felt as the world becomes globally smaller and nation states and people become more interdependent.[446] On the other hand, the fact that strong religious convictions exist throughout the world means that religion will continue to have significant impact on international law in each of their identified levels of interaction. The growing interest and wave of academic writing and court cases on the subject is a strong indication in this regard and is often ignored or overlooked at the international level.[447] Baderin argues that if international law is to achieve its aim of developing a legal framework that emphasises humanity and dignity in today's world, then international lawyers and academics can no longer afford to ignore the importance that religion plays for many people and many societies, simply because it can be predicted that it will continue to play that role in future.[448]

207. It would be for the benefit of both religion and international law and for the enhancement of humanity, if all, as human agents of both systems, strive to promote a friendly and harmonistic relationship between religion and international law rather than a belligerent or adversarial one.[449] This can be achieved by not downplaying the areas of difference between the two systems, but rather accentuating those areas of common ground and there must be a commitment to resolving possible areas of tension with good faith and with the principle that everything can be discussed.[450]

208. The principle of good faith is one of the implied terms found in all modern-day contracts, including the contract of employment between the employer and employee. According to the implied term of good faith, parties to the contract are

---

445. *Ibid.*
446. *Ibid.*
447. *Ibid.*, at 4.
448. S. Baderin, *From International Law of Christianity to the International Law of the Global Citizen* 3 JHIL 183 (2001).
449. *Ibid.*
450. *Ibid.*, at 184.

bound by everything which good faith reasonably and equitably demands.[451] This generally means that the parties to a contract will be acting in good faith and will not without reasonable or proper cause conduct themselves in a way that will destroy or seriously damage the relationship of trust and confidence between them.[452] Focus will now shift to the position of international law in relation to the protection and recognition of religious communities.

§3. The Position of International Law on Religious Freedom

209. International law just like domestic law has taken steps to guarantee the broader right of freedom to religion. The Universal Declaration of Human Rights (UDHR) states that all individuals have a right to freedom of thought, conscience and religion, including the freedom to change his or her religion or belief, and freedom, either alone or in community with others and in public or private, to manifest his or her religion or belief in teaching, practice, worship and observance.[453] This statement was incorporated into Article 18 of the International Covenant on Civil and Political Rights (ICCPR), which champions for the freedom of religion of an individual and collective and promotes the independence of religious communities in the international context.[454]

210. Though not embodied explicitly in other areas of international law, this right to free exercise of religion has been incorporated by reference into both the Genocide Convention and the Refugee Convention. Both Conventions include religious minorities among the kinds of groups that are protected by the convention. For example, the Genocide Convention criminalises acts committed with the intention to destroy, in whole or in part, a religious group or community.[455] While the Refugee Convention defines refugee as anyone who owing to a well-founded fear of being persecuted for reasons of religion is outside the country of his or her nationality or is unwilling to avail himself to the protection of that country.[456] While the Genocide and Refugee Convention protect minority groups, the 1970 United Nations Educational, Scientific and Cultural Organisation (UNESCO) Convention protects religious property through the protection of cultural heritage.[457] It is important to note that though the right to freedom of religion is codified in international conventions, it is unclear how this obligation is enforced through international courts.

451. M. Van Jaarsveld, *An Employees Contractual Obligation to Promote Harmonious Relationships in the Workplace – When are the Stakes too High? Some Pointers from the Judiciary*, 19 SA Mercantile Law Journal 205 (2007).
452. *Ibid.*
453. Article 18 UN UDHR 1948.
454. Article 18 ICCPR 1976.
455. Article 13 Genocide Convention 1948.
456. Article 2 Refugee Convention 1951.
457. Article 28 UNESCO Convention 1970.

211. For example, the Permanent Court of International Justice (PCIJ) dealt with the question of minority rights three times, in the case concerning the rights of minorities in Upper Silesia in 1928, in the advisory opinion concerning Greco-Bulgarian Communities in 1930 and in the court's advisory opinion concerning minority schools in Albania, issued in 1935.[458] In all three cases, the PCIJ established the obligation of countries to ensure de facto equality for minority religious communities. This de facto right included the right of a community to maintain its cultural identity, language and religion and to educate its children in its own schools.[459] In the case concerning the Rights of Minorities in Upper Silesia in 1928, the PCIJ was called to adjudicate a dispute between Poland and Germany arising out of a provision in the German-Polish convention which allowed minority religious communities in both countries to choose the language of instruction for their children.[460] The convention specifically applied to religious and linguistic minorities in Upper Silesia, a piece of territory divided between the two countries. The dispute arose because Polish authorities decided that around 7,000 children who had been enrolled in German-language schools in Upper Silesia were invalidly registered as religious or linguistic minorities and therefore had no right to attend schools established for German students under the convention.[461] The PCIJ dealt with this case under the Geneva Convention, which guaranteed every person the right to declare their affiliation to a linguistic or religious group. This is because the individual had the right to declare or not his or her affiliation to a minority religious or linguistic group, and his or her government did not have the right to review this declaration.[462] This standard was not designed to allow anyone to claim affiliation with any group solely to get a benefit. Instead, whether an individual belonged to a minority community and therefore is entitled to a benefit under law is a question of fact and not intention.[463] While a government may require an individual to provide some kind of proof of his stated affiliation, a government may not decide for itself which community an individual belongs to. The PCIJ applied this standard to Polish government's actions, saying that the protections of the Geneva Conventions were designed to avoid any kind of internal discrepancies within a government about the identification and classification of an individual.[464]

212. The concern was that this kind of discrepancy would lead to an individual being deprived of a benefit that he was entitled to as a member of a minority group. While this prohibition may lead to some individuals unjustly benefiting from a system designed to protect minorities, a government has to take this risk.[465] By reviewing and questioning the decisions made by individual parents to enrol their children

---

458. C.F. Amerasinghe, *The Permanent Court of International Justice and the International Court of Justice: Contentious Jurisdiction* 46 (International law E Books 2008).
459. *Ibid.*
460. *Ibid.*, at 47.
461. *Ibid.*
462. *Ibid.*
463. *Ibid.*, at 48.
464. *Ibid.*
465. *Ibid.*, at 49.

in minority schools, the Polish government violated the Geneva Convention's mandate.[466] In reaching this decision, the PCIJ treated religion as both a personal and collective right. Under the PCIJ's reasoning, religious minorities have the right to educate their children as they see fit. As such, minority communities have the right to establish institutions like schools and places of worship and this right is a collective one. In contrast, the right to freedom of religion is a personal one, since individuals have the right to decide which group they belong to. The individual, not the community or the government, has the right to be identified as a member of a minority community and to choose where and how his or her children are educated.[467] In this case and the other cases mentioned above that are dealt by the PCIJ in connection with the protection of religious communities in the international context, the PCIJ adopted a hybrid conceptualisation of the right to freedom of religion.[468] The court upheld this model of minority rights in 1930, in its advisory opinion concerning the rights of minority groups in Green and Bulgaria.[469] There, the court considered the obligations imposed by the two states by a bilateral reciprocal emigration treaty. As part of its decision, the court held that this communal right to religion, minority communities had the right to maintain their traditions and way of life.[470]

213. Unlike the PCIJ, the International Court of Justice (ICJ) has no explicit mandate to consider and adjudicate questions related to minority treaties or treaties related to cultural rights. As a result, the ICJ has seen a limited number of cases related to cultural rights and adopted a narrow approach when it comes to the interpretation of that particular right to religious communities.[471] Even though the ICJ has a narrow approach and limited jurisdiction when it comes to the recognition and promotion of religious communities, the role of both the PCIJ and ICJ can be summarised as follows as international organs which aim to protect religious communities. Though the PCIJ and ICJ have only considered the rights of minority religious groups in a handful of contexts, both courts have suggested that the right to freedom of religion is both an individual right based on an individual's conscience and a communal right, honoured as a way to protect a population's traditions and a way of life.[472] However, unlike its predecessor, the ICJ's rulings on this question has been narrower and to the detriment of religious communities in the international context. As such, the ICJ's jurisprudence has provided little actual protection to minority religious groups around the world, including those in states under the ICJ's jurisdiction. Litigation centred on protecting the cultural and religious rights of minority populations has largely taken place in domestic courts, meaning minority populations remain vulnerable legally.[473]

---

466. *Ibid.*
467. *Ibid.*
468. *Ibid.*, at 50.
469. *Ibid.*
470. *Ibid.*, 51.
471. G. Zyberi, *The International Court of Justice and the Rights of Peoples and Minorities*, 14 Series 2 (2013).
472. *Ibid.*
473. *Ibid.*, at 3.

§4. Religious Rights and Communal Protection by International Criminal Law

214. Unlike PCIJ and ICJ, the cases before international criminal tribunals, which touch on the rights of religious minorities, focus almost exclusively on the rights of minority communities to their religious cultural symbols, rather than the rights of the individual members of these minority communities.[474] The International Criminal Tribunal for the former Yugoslavia (ICTY) and ICC have both focused exclusively on the destruction of religious property and sacred sites during armed conflicts. In part, this focus is driven by the jurisdiction of the two tribunals – both tribunals assign criminal penalties to individuals who violate the laws of war and commit crimes of genocide or crimes against humanity. As such, cases before these bodies focus almost exclusively on acts committed by an individual or group of individuals against a group.[475] The cases before ICTY that relate to the rights of religious minority communities have focused almost exclusively on the allegations of plunder and excessive destruction of property, in violation of the laws and customs of war and the Geneva Conventions.[476]

215. Because of ICTY's role in prosecuting autocracies committed during armed conflict in the Balkans in the 1990s, the cases heard by the tribunal relating to minority rights focused primarily on the destruction of cultural and religious property. However, by saying that the intentional destruction of cultural and religious property constituted a violation of the laws and customs of war, the tribunal also articulated a version of minority rights based on the rights of a community to access houses of worship and its sacred shrines.[477] This right is identical to the one articulated by the ICJ in its advisory role relating to the wall on Palestinian territory. ICTY's jurisprudence combined with its advisory opinion from the ICJ suggest that the right of a minority population to preserve and access their sacred sites is protected through the protection of the sites themselves.[478] Like ICTY, ICC has only considered minority rights in the context of the prohibition against the international destruction of cultural and religious property. The ICC has considered this issue once in *Prosecutor v. Ahmad Al Faqi Al Mahdi*. In this case the court considered charges against A, an Islamic cleric who worked with Al Qaeda of the Islamic Maghreb (AQIM) in Mali to specifically target religious practices deemed contrary to AQIM teachings.[479] As part of this campaign A and others started to destroy religious sites of cultural and historical importance around Mali, including mausoleums and shrines.[480] The court held that this destruction constituted a war crime

474. A. Birdsall, *The International Criminal Tribunal for the Former Yugoslavia – Towards a More Just Order?*, 8 PCD 3 (2006).
475. *Ibid.*
476. *Ibid.*, at 4.
477. *Ibid.*
478. *Ibid.*, at 5.
479. *Prosecutor v. Ahmad Al Faqi Al Mahdi* 48 (ICC, 2016).
480. *Ibid.*

under Article 8(2) (e) (ii) of the Rome Statute, which prohibits attacks against civilian targets during armed conflicts.[481] The court also held that the attacks violated both the Geneva Convention and the Second Protocol to the Hague Convention, and as such constituted a criminal act within the court's jurisdiction.[482]

216. The court ultimately sentenced A to nine years in prison for the destruction of these monuments, holding that these crimes were committed with the intent to impose a specific religion on the population of Timbuktu through armed conflict.[483] The religious sites targeted were specifically protected by the UNESCO Convention and they were destroyed because of their cultural significance to the local people. As such A not only intended to traumatise the local population through a campaign of terror but he also intended to rob the population of religious and cultural symbols vital to its identity.[484] Despite ICC's holding in *Prosecutor*, similar cases heard by the ICTY is limited specifically to the destruction of religious monuments during war time; however, the court's rhetoric in the case suggests a broader conception of the protection of religious rights.[485] Like ICTY, the court focuses specifically on the right of a population to its cultural and historic sites, especially to shrines that have been part of the area's tradition and history for generations. However, the court also suggests that these acts become more serious when committed as part of a systematic programme of imposing religious beliefs on a population. This raises the possibility that, in the future, the court will be more willing to look into a country's practices relating to its treatment of minority religious groups.[486] However, the ICC's holding in *Prosecutor* is limited in a few important ways, which again suggest that the vast majority of protections afforded to religious minorities come from domestic rather than international law. First, *Prosecutor* rests with Article 8(2) (e) of the Rome Statute, which defines war crimes, meaning its holding is limited to the context of armed conflict. Therefore, *Prosecutor* cannot be used to target practices by world leaders during peacetime.[487] Second, the ICC's jurisdiction itself is limited by the Rome Statute and by the fact that it has a limited enforcement mechanism. So even if the ICC chooses to enquire more deeply into a state's policies with respect to its minority groups, it is unclear whether this enquiry will actually be meaningful or function as a way to protect minority populations.[488] Finally *Prosecutor* is currently the only case in which the ICC has charged and convicted someone for the destruction of cultural property, and it is unclear how and if the ICC's jurisprudence in this area will evolve in the future.

481. *Ibid.*
482. *Ibid.*, at 49.
483. *Ibid.*
484. *Ibid.*
485. *Ibid.*, at 50.
486. *Ibid.*
487. *Ibid.*
488. *Ibid.*, at 51.

§5. CONCLUSION

217. Though the UDHR and the International Convention on Civil and Political Rights articulate the right to freedom of religion as a deeply personal one, international tribunals, including the ICC, ICJ and ICTY have all conceptualised this right primarily as a communal one. These international tribunals have opted overwhelmingly to protect freedom of religion by protecting the rights of minority communities to educate their children and maintain access to their sacred sites. As a result, international law does very little work towards protecting the right to freely exercise of religion for minority communities outside the context of an armed conflict.

218. In part, this is due to the jurisdictional constraints placed on international tribunals. It is rare for a question concerning free exercise of religion to be heard by a body like the ICC or the ICJ outside the context of armed conflict, or at least hostility. This lack of protection is also driven by the conceptualisation of religion as a communal right, since it requires only that a community be allowed to exist, not that the individual members of the community be able to participate fully and freely in the political process. As a result, international law is fundamentally weak in the area of protecting and enforcing the ICCPR's mandate that every individual has the right to freedom of conscience, belief and culture.

Chapter 2. Transnational Law Effects on Religious Communities

§1. Introduction

219. International business transactions occur within a web of legal frameworks. Some are national, like the legal systems of the parties' countries, while others are international, like the legal systems created by various treaties or the rules of customary international law. Yet the division between national and international should not be overstated. In fact, as we shall see that international law penetrates and influences national systems in a variety of ways, while national laws and practices shape international law. To avoid misleading distinctions, Professor Philip Jessup (later a judge on the ICJ) proposed the phrase 'transnational law'. Jessup defined this phrase 'to include all law which regulates actions or events that transcend national frontiers. Both public and private international law are included, as are other rules which do not wholly fit into such standard categories'.[489] In the best of all possible intellectual worlds, the student of international business transactions would already have acquired a familiarity with international law and its relation to domestic legal systems in a course like Public International Law or Transnational Law. However, realism and experience suggest that this is not always the case. This chapter therefore introduces some of the concepts an international business lawyer must understand.

§2. Does Transnational Law Represent a New and Independent Legal Order

220. Transnational Law can be defined as the law of non-state governance systems. The definition suggests both commonalities and differences between 'transnational law' as a distinct legal field and conventional legal fields derived from the legal orders of nation states.[490] Like domestic law fields, transnational law includes both a constitutional element (a basic set of presumptive and supreme organising principles and rules), a substantive element (implementing the constituted system) and a process element (rules for the development of substantive rules and dispute resolution.[491] Unlike domestic legal orders, transnational law covers a wide number of distinct governance communities existing simultaneously and organised beyond the rule that imposes power of states. Moreover, these governance communities are not necessarily organised in the same way as states with a population and a defined geographic territory and an institutional framework exercising plenary authority.[492] Rather, transnational law communities may be understood as functionally differentiated communities organised for mutual benefit for specific objectives. They can include groups, institutions and networks. Transnational law can thus be understood as the study of the system of principles and rules applied in lieu of or in addition to

489. P. Jessup, *Transnational Law* 8 IGLP 1 (2012).
490. *Ibid.*, at 2.
491. *Ibid.*, at 3.
492. *Ibid.*, at 3.

the domestically germane law of a state, or of the community of states, to the relationships among persons and institutions.

§3. What Persons or Entities Control the Creation and Regulation of Transnational Law

221. No one person, entity or single institution controls transnational lawmaking. Transnational law is not dependant on a single lawgiver or regulator. Transnational law is thus the study of law that does not belong to, or can be controlled, by any single system of domestic or international law, as both have been traditionally constituted.[493] Diffusion of regulatory authority is one key to understanding the structure of Transnational lawmaking. Another key is functional differentiation of authority among a wide variety of political and non-political communities. The system of hierarchical and vertically integrated regulatory systems grounded on the state as the pinnacle of lawmaking and on the community of states as the disciplinary mechanism for relations among states has been augmented by regulatory systems covering matters beyond the reach of any single state.[494] Transnational law starts from the premise that law and lawmaking are no longer the exclusive preserve of political states, or of the community of states. Transnational law provides that political communities no longer hold a monopoly on lawmaking and that law systems are no longer grounded on an identity between law (or regulatory authority) and the state (and the community of states). Autonomous supra-national actors, private global actors and communities grouped by function or affinity can, to some extent, produce regulatory systems understood to be transnational, and this without a doubt includes both religious and cultural communities.

§4. Is Transnational Law a Single or Unitary System of Laws, Rules and Principles

222. Transnational law is not a unitary system of laws and rules analogous to the legal structure of a state, or the treaty and custom structure of the law of nations. Transnational law is an amalgam of rule systems, of hard and soft laws, that are limited in scope, but effective within the scope of the authority of the rulemaking community.[495] The key characteristic of transnational sub-systems is their functional limits. Like classical federal systems, all transnational sub-systems are based on grants of limited and specific authority. These limits are defined sometimes by commercial law, investment, human rights and sometimes by other factors such as shared belief, citizenship and in particular political communities and religion or culture in some instances.[496] The aggregation of sub-systems together constitutes the

---

493. *Ibid.*, at 4.
494. *Ibid.*
495. H.E. Foley, *Incorporation, Multiple Incorporation and the Conflict of Laws*, 42 Harvard Law Review 516 (2000).
496. *Ibid.*

field of Transnational law. However, Transnational law as a whole is grounded in certain principles and rules that form the basic focus of any study in this field. The foundational premise rests on acceptance of the existence independent of the control or authority of any one state or of the community of states of a system of non-national, supra-national or multi-national principles and rules applicable, in accordance with its own terms and logic, to public and private actors, natural and juridical persons.[497]

§5. What Are the Principal Features of the Study of Transnational Law

223. There are four characteristics that form the basis of the study of the grounding rules and principles of Transnational law and lawmaking: (1) scope of authority, (2) institutional autonomy, (3) regulatory authority and (4) effectiveness of power to settle disputes.[498] These have a constitutional element, the organising principles, that give the regulatory community form and set its organisational boundaries. These include the Constitution of a government apparatus and the rules for the operation of the governance with power vested in this organisation. They also have substantive and process elements.[499] These include the rules, laws and other norms that are produced or administered by the community and the process rules through which they are applied, enforced, constructed and interpreted. This is where religious and cultural communities fit in perfectly because they are independent and autonomous in the sense that they are in a position to determine their own rules and procedures. However, in the South African context this independence must be exercised in line with the prescripts of the Constitution, which is the supreme law of the land.

224. From the study and discussion of transnational law which in a nutshell deals with the personal laws of religious and cultural communities, in this case in the South African context. These personal laws aim to strengthen and build the religious and cultural communities from state inference. An example of legal rules or principles that can be viewed as Transnational law in this case is the L&D as outlined above, and as already discussed that such personal laws must be in line with the provisions of the Constitution.

§6. Conclusion

225. The independence and autonomy of religious and cultural organisations to establish rules and procedures in connection with their day-to-day operation and governance form part of Transnational law. The power of these religious and cultural bodies to establish their own rules and procedures forms part of the freedom

497. *Ibid.*, at 517.
498. *Ibid.*
499. *Ibid.*, at 518.

to choose religion or culture as protected by the Constitution. Furthermore, it is clear that Transnational law will strengthen democracy in the case of the diverse nature of the South African community and it is also subject to the Constitution.

Chapter 3. Regional Law Effects on Religious Communities

§1. Introduction

226. While the United Nations (UN) operates at an international level, there are also regional institutions that aim to promote human rights. These institutions produce regional treaties and declarations, for example Regional Human Rights Institutions. The European Commission (EU) on Human Rights and the European Court of Human Rights are responsible for applying the European Convention on Human Rights. The Inter-American Commission on Human Rights and the Inter-American Court of Human Rights apply the American Convention on Human Rights. The reports, recommendations and decisions that come from these bodies are very persuasive, and they have been referred to by domestic courts in interpreting various human rights provisions. In this chapter, we will focus on the African system. African Union (AU) is Africa's principal organisation for the promotion of socio-economic integration of the continent. The AU grew out of the Organisation for African Unity (OAU). The OAU was a regional body with multiple objectives, including ridding Africa of the legacy of colonisation and apartheid, as well as fostering social and economic co-operation among African states. In 1999, the Heads of States of the OAU issued the Sirte Declaration that called for the creation of the AU.[500] The AU's role in the African continent is to accelerate the political and socio-economic integration of the continent; to encourage international co-operation, taking into account the UN Charter and the UDHR; to promote and protect human rights in accordance with the African Charter and other relevant human rights instruments; to work with relevant international partners in doing away with preventable diseases and in promoting good health on the continent.[501] More about the role and importance of the AU will be outlined in this chapter and other legal instruments and organisations that aim to build and enhance regional law will be discussed.

§2. African Commission on Human and Peoples' Rights

227. The African Commission on Human and Peoples' Rights is the monitoring body for the African Charter on Human and Peoples' Rights. The African Commission aims to do the following in its monitoring process or system in the continent of Africa:

(a) To receive reports from state parties, interstate reports and individual complaints where there are serious abuses.
(b) It has the power to investigate abuses.

---

500. B. Andemicael, *The OAU and the UN: Relations Between the Organisation of African Unity and the United Nations* 34 (Africana, New York 1976).
501. *Ibid.*, at 38.

(c) It can bring these abuses to the attention of the Assembly of Heads of State and Government of the AU. After being informed of abuses, the Assembly may then request the Commission to make an in-depth study, and to present a report with conclusions and recommendations.[502]

228. It is clear that the African Commission on Human and Peoples' Rights in its monitoring process ensures that fundamental rights of people which include the right to choose religion and culture freely are protected from a Transnational law perspective. If it does indeed find some form of abuse it will escalate it to the mother body which is the AU to ensure that the abuse is corrected and the rule of law is upheld in the continent of Africa.

§3. Regional Agreements

I. The African Charter on Human and Peoples' Rights (African Charter)

229. The primary regional instrument for South Africa relevant to economic, social and cultural rights is the African Charter on Human and Peoples' Rights (African Charter). South Africa became a party to the African Charter in 1996. The African Charter includes the 'right to enjoy the best attainable state of physical and mental health' in Article 16. The Article goes on to provide: 'State Parties to the present Charter shall take the necessary measures to protect the health of their people and to ensure that they receive medical attention when they are sick.'[503]

230. It is important to note that when reading the African Charter progressive realisation and available resources are not mentioned. This suggests that the obligations of the state parties to fulfil a right and not just the minimum essential level of the right are immediate.[504] However, this was not the interpretation given to Article 16 by the African Commission in *Purohit and Moore v. The Gambia*.[505] Among other rights, this case also concerned the right to health for mental health patients. The Commission noted the dissimilarity between the wording of the right to health in the charter and the ICESCR, but interpreted the charter in line with the ICESCR. It read into Article 16 the qualifiers of available resources and progressive realisation.

231. Based on the problems that were encountered in the above-mentioned court case, it resulted in the development and drafting of the Abuja Declaration. The Abuja Declaration of 2001 was drawn up by the Heads of State and Government of the OAU (now AU). The declaration considered the HIV/AIDS pandemic: 'As a state of emergency in the continent. To this end, all tariff and economic barriers to

502. R. Murry, *Human Rights in Africa: From the OAU to the African Union* 5 (Cambridge University Press, Cambridge 2005).
503. Article 16 African Charter on Human and People's Rights 1986.
504. Section 27 of the Constitution.
505. *Purohit and Moore v. The Gambia [Communication 241/2001].*

access to funding of AIDS-related activities should be lifted.' The states committed themselves to: take all necessary measures to ensure that the needed resources are made available; mobilise all the human, material and financial resources required to provide care, support and quality treatment; and enact and use appropriate legislation and international trade regulations to ensure the availability of drugs at affordable prices.[506] From the drafting of this declaration and its adoption in the African continent it can be said that it was a vehicle for ensuring that a fundamental right which in this case was access to healthcare services is realised through making use of Transnational law. One can thus argue that Transnational law had a positive effect on the continent of Africa in fighting the HIV/AIDS pandemic due to co-operation and commitments of Member States.

II. African Court on Human and Peoples' Rights

232. In June 1998, the Protocol to the African Charter on Human and Peoples' Rights on the Establishment of the African Court on Human and Peoples' Rights (ACHPR) (the Protocol) was adopted by the OAU, the predecessor of the AU. Civil society and Non-governmental Organisations (NGOs) played an important role in the drafting and adoption of this Protocol. More than five years after the adoption of the Protocol, fifteen ratifications were achieved, and the Protocol took effect on 15 January 2004.[507]

233. At the time of writing, the ACHPR was in the process of being set up, despite a decision that was taken at an AU summit meeting in 2004 to merge the ACHPR with the African Court of Justice that has yet to be established. The merger raises complexities that threatened to delay the establishment of the ACHPR, but the AU decided that setting up the court is a priority, and it should not be delayed.[508] While human rights activists welcome the move to create the ACHPR, there are some concerns regarding the proposed manner of operation. For example, there are no clear rules as to how the ACHPR and the African Commission are to work in relation to each other, especially regarding the procedure for referring cases from the African Commission to the ACHPR. Another important concern is that the Protocol restricts access to the ACHPR by individuals and NGOs. State parties are required to sign a declaration that states that they recognise the competence of the ACHPR to receive complaints from NGOs.[509] If a state has not done this, the ACHPR will not be able to hear complaints against that state that are brought by NGOs. Further, only NGOs that have an observer status with the African Commission may file cases before the ACHPR.

234. Without a doubt, the establishment of the ACHPR is a good move for the continent of Africa, but it presents challenges as already outlined in ensuring that

506. Article 2 of the Abuja Declaration of 2001.
507. Article 2 of the ACHPR 2004.
508. Article 5 of the ACHPR.
509. Article 6 of the ACHPR.

fundamental rights of people are protected through easy access to the court as a first step. However, bearing in mind the colonial past of the entire continent of Africa, gradual progress is eminent and the same can be said with how the ACHPR operates; it is bound to change in the interest of all the people of Africa.

III. New Partnership for Africa's Development

235. New Partnership for Africa's Development (NEPAD) was adopted at the 37th session of the Assembly of Heads of State and Government in July 2001 in Lusaka, Zambia. NEPAD is an integrated development plan to address key social, economic and political priorities. It is meant to develop values and monitor their implementation within the AU to: promote accelerated growth and sustainable development; eradicate widespread and severe poverty; and halt the marginalisation of Africa in the globalisation process.[510]

236. Policy reform in the human development sector is a priority, and it focuses on health together with other areas, such as religion and cultural practices. Some of the health objectives of NEPAD are to:

(a) strengthen programmes for containing communicable diseases;
(b) achieve secure health systems that meet needs and support disease control effectively; and
(c) successfully reduce the burden of disease on the poorest people in Africa. NEPAD's action plans include strengthening Africa's participation in processes aimed at procuring affordable drugs and exploring the use of alternative delivery systems for essential drugs and supplies.[511]

237. NEPAD as a policy reform document aims to work hand in hand with the Abuja Declaration or even to strengthen it to a lesser or greater extent. This is because both legal instruments aim to ensure that access to healthcare services and other socio-economic rights are realised in the African continent with the necessary urgency.

IV. African Peer Review Mechanism

238. In July 2002, the African Peer Review Mechanism (APRM) was established at the 6th summit of the Heads of State and Government Implementation Committee of NEPAD. The APRM is a self-monitoring mechanism designed to track the progress and performance of Member States in their quest for democracy, human rights and good governance. The APRM's main aim is to foster the adoption of appropriate laws policies, standards and practices that lead to political stability

510. Article 1 of the NEPAD 2001.
511. Article 2 of the NEPAD.

and economic growth and integration.[512] The APRM does this through: sharing experiences; reinforcing successful and best practices; and reviewing the performance of particular countries – one of the four focus areas for review is socio-economic development.[513]

239. The APRM depends on Member States voluntarily agreeing to be reviewed. South Africa was one of the first countries to agree, and this process began in late 2005. The peers or fellow heads of states receive reports prepared by experts and make recommendations. However, they have no mandate to punish Member States that do not follow these recommendations.[514] However, there is pressure on participating states to achieve positive reports from the review team as the APRM influences donor organisations and countries on which countries should be favoured as funding recipients. This is a strong incentive for states to conform with NEPAD's values.[515]

V. Southern African Development Community

240. The Southern African Development Community (SADC), previously the Southern African Development Coordination Conference, was formed in April 1980, by nine southern African countries: Angola, Botswana, Lesotho, Malawi, Mozambique, Swaziland, Tanzania, Zambia and Zimbabwe. It has now expanded to a membership of fourteen countries, including South Africa.[516] One of SADC's aims is: 'to achieve development and economic growth, alleviate poverty, enhance the standard and quality of life of the peoples of Southern Africa and support the socially disadvantaged through regional integration'.[517] In 1997 SADC adopted the SADC HIV/AIDS and Employment Code. This Code has been used by NGOs to try to persuade governments to adopt legislation that is similar to the Code. The SADC Protocol on Health aims to improve the health of the population through close co-operation in the region, recognising that this is: 'essential for the effective control of communicable diseases, non-communicable disease and for addressing common health concerns'.[518] The Protocol aims to: promote activities that have the potential to improve health, such as the development of healthcare personnel and facilities; encourage co-operation with international partners; and help develop common strategies to address the needs of vulnerable groups.[519]

241. In August 2000, SADC approved the Principles to Guide Negotiations with Pharmaceutical Companies on provision of Drugs for Treatment of HIV/AIDS and related conditions in SADC Countries. SADC was making efforts to implement its

512. Article 2 of the APRM 2002.
513. Article 2 of the APRM.
514. Article 3 of the APRM.
515. Article 4 of the APRM.
516. Article 1 of the SADC 1980.
517. Article 2 of the SADC.
518. Article 3 of the SADC.
519. Article 4 of the SADC.

HIV and AIDS Strategic Programme and Plan of Action 2003–2007, and this plan has been implemented in 2019 in order to reach more people.

§4. Conclusion

242. In conclusion, it is very much clear that from a continental perspective Africa is making serious inroads in ensuring that fundamental rights are upheld and protected. This is through the adoption of various legal instruments as discussed and also the various tribunals or forums that implement and protect the said rights as enshrined in the various declarations as part of Transnational law. Despite some of the challenges, Africa is without a doubt in the right direction and Transnational law makes it easy for all the fifty-four countries in Africa to co-operate and work together as a unit, with the aim of bringing the necessary social cohesion to the people of Africa. Focus will now be on exploring the relationship between religion and politics in South Africa, bearing in mind the close relationship that is shared by both religion and politics in the struggle against apartheid.

Part V. Religion and Politics

Chapter 1. Influence of Religion in Politics

§1. Introductions

243. The history of religion and politics in South Africa is fundamental and important. This can be attributed to the important role religion played in the development of political consciousness in South Africa with the sole purpose of ensuring that apartheid comes to an end. Religion was also used as one of the mechanisms to oppress the majority of black people, by imposing a foreign religion on local people and forcing them to abandon their own religion and culture in the process. This meant that for the liberation of the black majority in South Africa, it was without a doubt necessary to make use of the very same religion to end the evil apartheid era.

244. Religion provided the necessary space and resources through the various church organisations in South Africa with the sole purpose of ensuring that the people of South Africa are free from political oppression. This is the reason why in this chapter it is argued that religion is fundamental in the democratic dispensation of South Africa. The role and importance of religion will be discussed in the chapter with the sole aim of outlining the historical links or importance which are shared by both religion and politics in South Africa today, post-1994.

§2. The Role of Religion in Politics

245. The role of religion in politics is a topic that has gained enormous significance in light of the events of 11 September 2001. It has left almost everyone thinking that religion in politics is probably negative, harmful and something to be avoided, especially the events in New York and Washington exemplify the negative role of religion while operating in the political sphere.[520] I say this without presuming any particular upswing by the dominant discourse. I fear that the discourse that we are engaged in currently has the potential to create an atmosphere in which religion is simply disqualified from any role in politics. This is very difficult for generations of activists who found a comfortable intersection between religion and

520. *September 11 Terror Attacks Fast Facts*, https://edition.cnn.com/2013/07/27/us/september-11-anniversary-fast-facts/index.html (accessed 2 Aug. 1988).

politics.[521] Therefore, focus will be on experiences of religion and politics in South Africa not as a representative of a political party, but as a co-religionist. It is very difficult to accept that religion should be disqualified from any political role, even potentially. It is very clear that the role of religion in politics up to 1994 was fairly undisputed.[522] On the one hand, one finds the NG Kerk, theologically justifying apartheid, helping to present the apartheid state as Christian, but creating no distinction between what it saw as Christian values and the need for the apartheid state to be the abode of these particular values.[523] This was the major form of discourse on religion and politics. Against this, across racial, religious and denominational lines, there were three broad responses to the apartheid state.

246. First, it was the accomodationist response, which consisted largely of traditional orthodox and conservative elements, not very active in opposing apartheid but simply carrying on with life. Second, it was the response of those who represented and adopted religious discourse to challenge apartheid, reaching a high point with the development of a liberation theology and where religious figures became active partners in the struggle, making contributions that often ranged from simple prayer right up to martyrdom. Third, and lastly, the response to the apartheid state in the pre-1994 period was far more fundamentalist.[524] It was a hybrid fundamentalism rather, sometimes operating in the realm of traditional orthodoxy and at other times reflecting aggressive evangelism and an aggressive relationship with God as the antidote to evil that goes on in society. This strand within the challenging discourse argued that what we are busy with is not the formation of a democratic South Africa, but an Islamic or theocratic state.[525] They thus put the margins a little bit further than what the broad spectrum of people in South Africa were busy with. The liberation theology discourse was in a sense hegemonic. It had powerful charismatic advocates, a coaching theology and popular appeal, but its projection was often disproportionate to its actual size. In the Muslim community the few acted as a fig-leave for the many. A similar situation was often projected in Christian theology as well, as if all Christians were active in the anti-apartheid struggle.[526]

247. The truth is that those who were opponents of apartheid hid their marginal status because of the need to create the illusion of a mass popular theological uprising against apartheid. This is the first instance where forgiveness should be asked for in advance. The post-apartheid, post-1994 construction of a democratic state effectively displaced the focused role of religion in politics so prevalent in the apartheid era at the intellectual, theological and philosophical level.[527] It was replaced

---

521. H. Bredekamp & R. Ross, *Missions and Christianity in South African History* 14 (Wits University Press 1995).
522. *Ibid.*, at 15.
523. W. Saayman, *Being Missionary, Being Human: An Overview of Dutch Reformed Mission* 12 (Cluster Publications 2007).
524. *Ibid.*, at 13.
525. J. Kruger, *The Human Search for Meaning: A Multi-Religious Introduction of the Religions of Humankind* 42 (National Book Printers 1996).
526. *Ibid.*, at 43.
527. *Ibid.*, at 44.

by ambiguity, confusion and demobilisation of religious forces and of the religious discourse in politics. The key debates that emerged at the time centred on the new role of the church or of religion in post-apartheid South Africa.[528] Some church leaders felt that now that the real political leaders were free, the priests should return to the parish. The church should now get on with the business of religion and politicians should take on the business of politics.

248. Without a doubt the model-building that was done up to 1994 eroded in that moment of ambiguity, confusion and demobilisation. The impact of this ambiguity resulted in the return of the dichotomy between religion and politics. Church activists were recalled to the parish, resulting in an abdication by intellectuals from the project to transform South Africa. This abdication was a product of the discourse at the time of 1994, which still prevails until today.[529] This discourse centred on the question of the essential nature of the democratic state in the post-1994 period. The answer to that question, which is now the dominant and hegemonic position, is that the essence of democracy is opposition; if you don't have an opposition, you don't have a democracy. The alternative to the same question, which is far less than hegemonic, is that the essence of democracy in a post-apartheid, post-polarised, unequal, damaged society has to be transformation.[530]

249. It is not suggested that there must be a creation of three walls between the two options: either choose or oppose transformation. The argument is that the consequence of the idea of opposition as the central thesis of democracy has resulted in the pronouncement that the church has only one role politically, and that is to be the watchdogs of society.[531] One can understand where the dominant discourse comes from because it speaks to the sentiments of a group who have enjoyed all the power and privilege up to 1994, and who are now set up as the opposition. They therefore see opposition as the essence of democracy.[532] It speaks to the discourse of a group who understood that quick transformation was to be the essence of a democratic project to which they had to contribute, and therefore, it was not comfortable to say that the essence of democracy is transformation. It was far better to say that the essence of democracy is opposition, with all its racial assumptions, and that a black government should not be trusted.[533] It is argued that the Constitution was precisely crafted in a way to facilitate the ongoing contribution of religion to politics. When the Constitution was conceived and when it came to discussion on the relationship between state and religion, there were four options.

250. There was the option that we should craft an atheistic state, hostile to religion, a state that had nothing to do with religion or did not encourage it. This option

528. Saayman, *supra* n. 524, at 15.
529. Bredekamp & Ross, *supra* n. 522, at 16.
530. *Ibid.*
531. *Ibid.*, at 17.
532. Saayman, *supra* n. 524, at 16.
533. *Ibid.*

would have been betrayal because the very nature of South African society is fundamentally religious.[534] It would also betray the entire role that religion played in bringing us to freedom. Therefore, this option never really became an issue of discussion in our work towards our new Constitution.[535] Then there were obviously those who thought that maybe this is the moment to craft a theocratic state. South Africa has its own problems in terms of its diversity and it was not necessary to encourage this kind of discourse because it simply involved too many complications.[536] The third option was to construct a secular state where religion operated in the private sphere, where individuals believe what they choose, as long as there is tolerance of the religious sentiments of other people.[537] The option that was eventually adopted and that's placed in the Constitution is one of the secular state, but with an active role for religion, that guarantees freedom and even guarantees access to resources in order to make sure that religions are equitably represented.[538]

251. For example, town planning should make sure that religious sites are made available equitably, the airwaves and television time have to be proportionally allocated, etc.[539] The Constitution guarantees equality of status for all religions, but for proportion of facility, i.e., you don't have Muslims and Christians sharing equal time on radio since their demands are different. What is disappointing is that the broader religious community did not take up this discourse and therefore the fourth position was not debated.[540] Important questions concerning challenges and responsibilities were not raised. What we had was religion claiming its rights. The question to be asked is whether the religious establishments fulfilled their responsibility because the Constitution did not simply guarantee religious freedom; it also offered an opportunity for religious activism.

252. No one seems to be crafting a theology of transformation to guide and bring the people of South Africa together, as was the case with the theology of liberation in the apartheid years. A theology of transformation, for example, should be able to help in influencing and guiding the debate on whether South Africa is indeed a country of two nations, one, rich and white and the other, poor and black.[541] In this way, it isn't a matter of simple political discourse about what exists or not, or whether the former President of South Africa Thabo Mbeki is right or wrong. There must be some objective value to ensure that we are guided by in our scriptures, so that we speak with conscience and not simply with the pragmatism of the

534. T. Masuku, *Prophetic Mission of Faith Communities During Apartheid South Africa, 1948–1994: An Agenda for a Prophetic Mission Praxis in the Democratic South Africa*, 42 Missionalia 4 (2014).
535. *Ibid.*
536. *Ibid.*, at 5.
537. *Ibid.*
538. Section 15(1) of the Constitution.
539. Saayman, *supra* n. 524, at 17.
540. *Ibid.*
541. Masuku, *supra* n. 535, at 6.

moment.[542] We thus begin to spell out the complementary roles of politics and religion, without holding that religious activists should be politicians, or that politicians should be religious activists, or that they all have the same role. Politicians in South Africa often operate on a pragmatic basis in which tasks are mediated with the idea and the identification of one country and two nations. Religion asserts values; it asks questions of right and wrong, of practical implementation, of fulfilling God's command.[543]

253. Religion, for example, consults scripture on our role in persuading those who have to share and those who have not to be patient until the sharing starts taking effect. The absence of a theology of transformation creates an intellectual gap in society.[544]

254. The role of religion in addressing equality and freedom in South Africa in the current democratic dispensation is something that cannot be underestimated, but is very crucial. Religion has to confront its own ideological debates and try to fashion a broad consensus and coherence that is once again hegemonic.[545] Not all religious people were against apartheid, but those who were managed to occupy a position of hegemony in the 1993/1994 period. Therefore, it stands to reason that not all religious institutions will embrace transformation, but those that do must become hegemonic. To achieve this religion must overcome ideological divides and confront those within the broader religious community because the dominant discourse is still the traditional conservative orthodox one.[546]

255. Raymond Williams is correct in saying that orthodoxy cannot push back boundaries; it merely confirms.[547] Religion need to go beyond practicing a discourse that emerges in vicious form from time to time. Fundamentalist discourse avoids the real challenges of society by operating at the soft underbelly of an emerging democracy, taking on issues such as abortion, homosexuality, prostitution and crime to name but a few. Antonio Gramsci explains that transitions are the most painful and dangerous periods in the life of a nation because the old is not yet dead and the new has not yet been born.[548] When you have the old and the new coexisting so uncomfortably in society, you always have a powder keg. The discourse in religion that only seeks to ignite that powder keg does not confront the need to be the best undertakers or the worst of the old, and the midwives for the best of the new. South Africa need to bring about a discourse that hopefully starts to position religion as the undertaker of the worst and the midwife of the best. South Africa may not be able to convert everyone to this discourse, which some call post-modernist, others progressive. The point is that a new discourse must be hegemonic, due to the pluralistic nature of the South African community.

542. *Ibid.*
543. *Ibid.*, at 7.
544. *Ibid.*
545. *Ibid.*, at 8.
546. *Ibid.*
547. R. Williams, *Keywords: A Vocabulary of Culture and Society* 16 (Fontana 1976).
548. A. Gramsci, *Architect of a New Politics* 157 (Louisiana University Press 1990).

§3. CONCLUSION

256. From the discussion above it is clear that religion and politics are central to the new democratic dispensation of South Africa. Furthermore, as outlined above in relation to the important role of religion in society, it is very important to note that religion in its efforts of bringing social cohesion must also play a central role to the transformation debate of South Africa. This with the aim of ensuring that equality and freedom is also attained by religious organisations, as protected by the Constitution and bearing in mind the painful past which South Africa comes from, which is something that cannot be underestimated in the new democratic order.

Chapter 2. Political Influence in Religion

§1. Introduction

257. The close relationship between politics and religion in South Africa is one of the factors that shows political influence on religion to a lesser or greater extent. Political leaders in the past resorted to religion or churches for political support and liberation, bearing in mind that most political leaders have a religious background which was the position even during the apartheid era. Political leaders can influence religious communities and churches by providing donations and often visiting these churches or communities with the aim of growing political power and support in that particular community or church.

258. Politicians will go to the various churches with the aim of pulling the church members to vote for them during elections. This means that they will go and influence church members of a certain religious domination either to put them in power or to keep them in power come election period. Most of the people in South Africa who are part of religious dominations are poor and socio-economically disadvantaged and these politicians have exploited them to such an extent that they will promise service delivery to these vulnerable people before elections, but after elections do the opposite. This has resulted in serious consequences for politicians in recent times in a sense that violent service delivery protests around South Africa are taking full steam against politicians who lie to the general masses and use religion to gain cheap political points. The political influence on religion can best be described as a double-edged sword in which if this relationship is handled with care and honesty it can be prosperous to the entire community and politicians, in order to attain social cohesion. However, if this relationship is abused, which is often the case, then it will be detrimental, resulting in some cases lives being lost during service delivery protests. In addition, members of the religious community will lose trust in the government and not engage in democratic processes like going to vote and this without a doubt will be detrimental to the young democracy of South Africa, which cannot be separated from the importance of religion.

§2. The Intersection Between Religion and Politics

259. Focus will now be on the intersection of politics and religion through the lens of African traditional religion. African traditional religion which is most widely practiced among the indigenous people of South Africa is rich in diversity.[549] All religious dominations worship a supreme being, and in this case is the ancestors. This belief system accepts all other religions as equally valid constructions of

549. Mndende, *supra* n. 84, at 16.

knowledge and does not pretend to hold all the answers to human problems. Other views are considered, and often adopted, making African traditional religion a dynamic institution.[550]

260. Because African traditional religion believes that all authority eventually comes from the spirit world, any expression of power necessarily has religious implications. This principle manifested itself in several ways in the traditional Zulu culture, and it continues to surface in the current politics of Africa.[551] Religion was used to explain political failures and occupied the place of the political system in stateless societies. It also explains the tension over land ownership in modern southern Africa. Religion was employed in pre-colonial southern Africa to conceptualise the divide between good and evil in society.[552] Evil typically centred on the misuse of power. In societies where political institutions have abused the authority vested in them, religious discourse can be seen as an attempted remedy by means of reordering of power.[553] Religion was used to explain political misfortune in the community. Ngwabi Bhebe proposes that some Shona groups blamed their downfall on a former ruler who had abandoned traditional beliefs.[554] The ancestors sought to punish him and thus allowed the Zulu conquerors to triumph. In the same manner, when the king of Ndebele land, Lobengula, failed to hold off white invaders in the late nineteenth century, it was said that he received messages from Mwari, the Shona deity, claiming that the colonisers were actually Mwari's sons sent to punish Lobengula for excessive raiding of the Shona people.[555] In more recent times, the link between spiritual evil and political failure is still evident. A popular story in the Democratic Republic of Congo constructs an underground world where demons construe evil plans leading to the destruction of Africa. Using religious imagery, devilish creatures are depicted in modern situations, even with an underground international airport for all sorts of sorcerers and magicians flying in and out, and with various evil characters equated to World Bank and International Monetary Fund (IMF) agents.[556] Thus, a religious story is used to explain disillusionment over domestic political and economic processes and international political development and equate political failure with evil.

261. Similarly, religion often replaced central authority in early stateless societies. Religious structures and hierarchies translated into political organisers. This is known as authority over the spiritual world and thus translated into authority over people, making religion an outstanding means of instrumental sing political

550. *Ibid.*
551. *Ibid.*, at 17.
552. *Ibid.*
553. *Ibid.*, at 18.
554. B. Ngwabi, *The Historical Dimensions of Democracy and Human Rights in Zimbabwe* 16 (Mambo Press 2001).
555. *Ibid.*
556. *Ibid.*

power.[557] The use of lineage and clans, which continues today in indigenous communities, concentrates authority in the most senior living descendant. Different religious sects may also function as political factions, sects may counterbalance central authority, and by developing an ideology and relating particular actions and mundane practices within a wider set of meanings leading to a more honourable and dignified complexion to social conduct. Here, religion offers an alternative to the typical political process, and still achieves the same end, a more organised and accessible society.[558]

262. With this strong foundation in religion, different members of traditional African societies were able to manipulate religion for political purposes. Bhebe points out that when Zulu King Mzilikazi conquered the Shona in southern Zimbabwe he adopted many of their religious beliefs in order to integrate the Shona into Ndebele land peacefully for the political benefit of his kingdom.[559] Simultaneously, the Shona religious authorities were trying to curry favour with the new rulers by accepting them as God-sent.[560] With the beginnings of Christianity in Africa, and the creation of African Independent Churches, this same theme was evident. Africans appropriated certain aspects of Christianity that seemed politically beneficial yet maintained their traditional ritual practices. When the Christian missionaries gained strength during the colonial period, however, Africans allowed for more Christian customs in order to negotiate with the white conquerors.[561] In this way religion was used as a means to political stability and prosperity. Likewise, religious communities acted as targets for political mobilisation. By declaring authority from a supreme being, African rulers could demand taxes, labour or participation in the army.[562]

263. The most drastic mixing of religion and politics occurs when the line between the two is erased entirely. The belief that everything derives power from the spiritual world allows religion to actually usurp politics. Politicians or tribal rulers then come to rely on religion for their very legitimacy.[563] Religion determines power relationships and commercial ties, and thus it becomes the main institution in society. When Ndebele King Mzilikazi moved his Zulu followers out of South Africa and into Zimbabwe, conquering and incorporating groups as he went, he eventually found himself in an unfamiliar territory. This threatened his power because, as the king, he was responsible for appealing to his ancestors for rain for his people. However, his careful study of the clouds in South Africa was useless in Zimbabwe.[564] The Shona, whom he conquered in Zimbabwe, were experts in the Zimbabwean clouds and told Mzilikazi that if he appeased Mwari (the Shona deity) with black oxen, tobacco and other useful things, he could cause a downpour even

557. *Ibid.*, at 17.
558. *Ibid.*
559. *Ibid.*
560. *Ibid.*, at 18.
561. *Ibid.*
562. *Ibid.*, at 19.
563. *Ibid.*
564. Mndende, *supra* n. 84, at 18.

though there might be a drought.[565] Mzilikazi thus adopted the Shona belief in Mwari to maintain his political power. Moreover, a succession crisis followed Mzilikazi death, and a council was chosen to select the next king. Their leader, Mncumbata, appealed to Mwari for help, who directed him to Lobengula, Mzilikazi's son. Thus, the new king remained to some extent dependent on Mwari for his power to rule the Ndebele and their subjects. Lobengula's authority rested on the Ndebele's belief in Mwari, the traditional Shona God.[566]

264. Religion is able to manipulate politics because traditional African religion incorporates the spiritual world to such a high degree in everyday life. The ancestors are just as important as the people of the human world are. In this sense, the evolving political language of Africa tends to regard politics as a metaphor for movements in a spirit world rather than *vice versa.* Because the ancestors are the cause of evil and suffering, they also hold the key to peace and happiness.[567] All religious, and therefore political, communication is directed towards this end. Thus, the only way to attain political power is through the ancestors.

265. Recent religious revival in Africa demonstrates the prevalence of political and religious interdependence. At a time when political failure is widespread, coupled with the disillusionment of World Bank and IMF programmes for development, rekindled religious sentiment reflects disappointment with the current system of governance. Because religion locates evil in society, and allocates power accordingly, ambiguity concerning the morality of the state logically breeds religious excitement.[568] The same applies to nations with strong governments like South Africa. Here, religious movements challenge the very basis of legitimacy of states which operate through institutions and norms of governance originally created in colonial times. A considerable factor in the anger over forced removals under the apartheid regime stems from traditional religious beliefs. On the Zulu homestead, a clan's land is regarded as sacred. Ancestors are buried there, and it is also the site of important rituals. By forcing people to leave their lands, the central beliefs of African traditional religion were placed under direct attack by the state.[569]

266. Before the bureaucratic institutions established by colonial powers took form, religious specialists played an integral role of checking the chief or central authority figure to guard against corruption and tyranny. This concept has not faded with modernisation and education, as many Africans today continue to hold beliefs derived from traditional cosmologies which they apply to their everyday activities. In the contemporary African mind, concepts concerning ancestral interference with daily life still hold a considerable amount of influence. Instead of trying to eliminate or disregard such customs, international donors and developers must work within this unique African framework to find solutions to the continent's problems.

565. *Ibid.*
566. *Ibid.*, at 19.
567. *Ibid.*
568. *Ibid.*, at 20.
569. *Ibid.*, at 21.

§3. The Importance of Religion and Politics from a Perspective of Politicians in South Africa

267. 'Politics can do with the influence of the church.' Mmusi Maimane, the leader of Democratic Alliance (DA), which is the official opposition in South Africa, said this during his Good Friday address at the Faith Ways Bible Church in Soweto: 'You might be thinking why politicians are coming to churches, that it must be elections,' he said, 'I hold the belief that politics can do with the influence of the church. I still hold the belief that even those who founded the ANC were committed Christians.'[570]

268. He told congregants to 'look forward', and they murmured in agreement. 'It is time for us to say that we know where we come from. We are going to cross this Red Sea.'[571] Earlier on that day, former President Jacob Zuma called on Christians to pray for politicians, as the devil was trying to interfere with their work.[572]

269. He spoke to thousands of members of the Universal Church of the Kingdom of God at Ellis Park Stadium in Johannesburg. Zuma called on the congregants to pray for members of parliament to behave and conduct themselves in a respectful manner. He professed his love for the church and said the atmosphere in the stadium made him want to attend church regularly.[573] In KwaZulu-Natal, Premier Senzo Mchunu said the building of a stronger province would not succeed without religious leaders' involvement.[574] Senzo argued that churches must remain focused on their work of healing the nation and fighting injustices at all times.[575]

270. A prominent aspect in the speech of Senzo was when he said churches should criticise government when they felt it was going astray and failing to meet the expectations of society. He invited religious leaders to pray for a prosperous province.[576] Furthermore, Archbishop Thabo Makgoba of Cape Town called on government officials 'to tell the truth' about the Gupta family's alleged influence on matters of state capture. The Dominican Order of Catholic priests asked Public Protector Thuli Madonsela to investigate the Gupta's alleged involvement in ministerial appointments.[577] These few recent incidents in the South African position affirm that a strong relationship exists between religion and politics, and it is something that cannot be underestimated at all. Religion is instrumental and fundamental in the development of the new South Africa. This is affirmed by the participation of various political leaders in churches across the length and breadth of South Africa, to

570. *Why Is the Church a Non-player in Politics*, https://mg.co.za/article/2016-03-23-why-the-church-is-a-nonplayer-politically (accessed 14 Aug. 2018).
571. *Ibid.*
572. *Ibid.*
573. *South African Political Parties Go to Church*, https://www.news24.com/elections/news/sa-political-parties-go-to-church-20140420 (accessed 16 Aug. 2018).
574. *Ibid.*
575. *Ibid.*
576. *Ibid.*
577. *Ibid.*

seek spiritual intervention in cases where political solutions are not available in pursuit of building a prosperous South Africa.

§4. Conclusion

271. Religion and politics are dependent on each other and must work together in order to achieve the desired society in South Africa. This is the reason why politicians often visit churches across the country with the aim of growing their spirituality and also to seek for the intervention of the church in some instances to resolve a societal problem. This is taking place because both politicians and churches strive for the best interests of the people of South Africa, and to achieve this they must work together even though at times they might encounter some conflicts between them.

Chapter 3. Interaction Between Religion and State on a Political and Legal Level

§1. Introduction

272. The rich history that is shared by both religion and politics during the colonial and apartheid era has had a profound effect on the development and influence of the South African legal system. This in a nutshell means that basically the supreme law of the land in the form of the Constitution had to be developed to embrace diversity and to accommodate religion and religious communities. Law had to ensure that there is equality in South Africa, without any form of discrimination and maltreatment on all the inhabitants of South Africa, which was unfortunately the position in the past.

273. However, it is important to note that even though politics and religion had a profound effect on the development of the South Africa legal system, this does not mean that the judiciary has lost its independence and impartiality. The South African judiciary as one arm of the government is independent from political and religious interference, and it is only accountable to the Constitution as the supreme law of the land. One can argue that the close relationship between politics, religion and law from a historical perspective is aimed at ensuring that social cohesion is achieved and maintained, and that law is used as an instrument to determine the process or manner in which this social cohesion is achieved in a way that is fair and just in the interest of ensuring that no human rights are sacrificed at the expense of the other. This chapter explores as to how law, religion and politics operate with the aim of ensuring that social cohesion is maintained and how is the balancing exercise between the three spheres achieved in the interest of the religious community in this context.

§2. Religion and Law in South Africa

274. It is clear that in South Africa, like in the many places in which modernity was introduced through colonialism and missions, modernisation was not accompanied by an increasing level of atheism.[578] Quite the contrary; Christianity is a significant part of both our colonial and apartheid histories. It is clear that in terms of the fates of personal faith, South Africa has been a deeply religious country – religious in African customary terms, in Christianity and a significant minority of other religious traditions – particularly Islam, Hinduism and Judaism.[579] Religion has also been very significant to public and political life. The apartheid regime politicised Christianity in a number of ways through the National Party's close association with the Dutch Reformed Church, through apartheid's political theology of race and through Christian national education. Opposition to apartheid also drew heavily on

578. Mndende, *supra* n. 84, at 18.
579. *Ibid.*

Christianity. The development of liberation theology in the 1970s gave a platform to the Christian and Muslim leaders in the 1980s when they became politically active as the state cracked down on the leadership of civic and political organisations.[580]

275. The negotiations that framed South Africa's new democracy also paid attention to the place religion does, and ought to, take in the country. The negotiators acknowledged the importance of religion to the majority of South Africans and the variety of religious traditions in the country. The 1996 Constitution includes a strong right to freedom of religion, and the possibility of the presence of religion in state institutions under conditions of fairness and neutrality. Various forms for customary religious marriages are also provided for.[581] The drafters of the Constitution were also very clear to exclude reference to Christianity in the Preamble, and emphasised the importance of state neutrality towards various religions in law. During important state events, religious leaders of a variety of traditions play a role. At the same time, the TRC and political rhetoric often draw on the legacy of liberation theology.

§3. Politics and Law in South Africa

276. Politicians and the government of the day in South Africa also subscribe to the Constitution as the supreme law of the land. This means that the leader of a political party, for example the ANC president in South Africa, is also the president of South Africa. In taking the oath of office the president pledges that he or she will uphold the oath of office and respect the rule of law of the Republic and also encourage people to follow the rule of law.[582] Failure by the president to uphold this oath of office will constitute a gross violation of the Constitution, and he or she will be impeached from office on the basis of his or her failure to uphold his or her oath of office as the first citizen of the Republic.[583] This implies that the president as the first citizen is the one that must be the first defender of the Constitution and lead by example in ensuring that the rule of law is upheld and protected all the time.

277. Political parties in South Africa that exist because it is a multi-party democracy are also bound by the rule of law of the Republic. This means that the various political parties and their leaders cannot engage in practices which will put the Republic in danger such as to incite violence or criminality as this will be contrary to the laws of the Republic.[584] Such conduct by political parties and their leaders will be condemned as criminality, and they could face arrest and prosecutions in some instances for defying the law and aiming to bring chaos in the Republic of South Africa. Just like church organisations, political parties are also autonomous

580. *Ibid.*, at 19.
581. Section 15 of the Constitution.
582. Section 83 of the Constitution.
583. Section 89 of the Constitution.
584. Section 44 of the Constitution.

in the sense that they can develop their own Constitution or Code of Conduct which their members are expected to subscribe to it. However, such Constitution or Code of Conduct must not be contrary to the Constitution of the Republic in such a way that it is found to be discriminatory against certain groups of people. If this is found to be the case then such a Constitution or Code of Conduct will be found to be void and not in the interest of the administration of justice.[585]

278. Political parties and leaders are also bound by the court decisions or judgments that are given by the courts, and must ensure that they are implemented and not defied by them as they can face penalties such as contempt of court.[586] This means that political parties and their leaders must be exemplary all the time when it comes to ensuring that the rule of law is upheld and protected. Political leaders must encourage their members to be citizens that respect the rule of law because failure to do so has severe consequences for those leaders that aim to defy the law.[587] Such a duty rests with political parties due to the close relationship they enjoy with members of the public on the ground, and they are duty bound to ensure that their members are disciplined and are always on the right side of the law.

279. Political parties just like church organisations in South Africa, despite being autonomous, also face internal or external legal problems that threaten their existence or affect their reputation in South Africa. For example, political parties of recent times in South Africa have resorted to courts to resolve their internal disputes or for the court to assist them with the interpretation of their internal Code of Conduct or Constitution because such legal instruments will all the time be tested by the Constitution of the Republic as the supreme law.[588] This affirms the role and importance of the judiciary in South Africa because they not only provide legal certainty but go beyond to bring the necessary political certainty with the involvement and interpretation of the law. It is one of the major reasons why political parties and their leaders in South Africa must ensure that the rule of law is protected and upheld at all costs because law plays an important part in ensuring that even political problems which do not have political solutions are resolved through legal intervention and interpretation.

280. Politicians and political parties are not exempted from the rule of law. They are in fact the people that must guard and protect the rule of law. This will be possible by encouraging their members and the general public about the role and importance of the rule of law in the current democratic dispensation of South Africa. The future of the South African democracy lies with a collaboration between political, religious and law, working together with the aim of ensuring that social cohesion is achieved through embracing diversity and respecting the Constitution as the supreme law post-colonial and apartheid South Africa.

---

585. Section 2 of the Constitution.
586. Section 41 of the Constitution.
587. Section 42 of the Constitution.
588. Section 2 of the Constitution.

§4. CONCLUSION

281. South Africa as a pluralistic society requires a joint venture between law, religion and politics in ensuring that societal peace and growth are maintained at all costs. Furthermore, since law, religion and politics have an important role to play in a unique manner with the purpose of ensuring that the democracy of South Africa grows and succeeds on a daily basis, it is something that cannot be underestimated and must be protected. If there is a conflict between politics and religion which is often the case, law will come in with the role of a regulator and protector, to aim to resolve the said conflict in the public interest. While bearing in mind that religious and political institutions are autonomous and independent.

Part VI. Labour Law Within Religious Communities

Chapter 1. Scope of Application of Labour Law

§1. Introduction

282. The Constitution of South Africa was adopted on 10 May 1996 and came into effect on 4 February 1997. This means that the scope of application of the Constitution of South Africa is very vast, and it is not restricted to religious freedom and culture which is the focus in this regard. However, the constitutional application extends to the relationship between an employer and employee with the sole aim of safeguarding a fundamental right which is enjoyed by everyone, which is the right to choose an occupation or trade freely as protected by the Constitution.[589] This means that the Constitution aims to play a role of ensuring that there is fair labour practices that are taking place in the labour market, without any form of exploitation and discrimination.

283. The role of the Constitution in the labour market and the various statutory provisions which deal with labour matters will be explored in this chapter, with the aim of exposing the importance and significance of the labour market that if it is unregulated it can result in dire consequences.

§2. Labour Rights in the Constitution

284. The Constitution contains a Bill of Rights, which enshrines the rights of all South Africans, and reference will now only be made to labour rights as the theme of this chapter. The following labour rights are enshrined in the Constitution:

(a) everyone has the right to fair labour practices;
(b) every worker has the right to form and join a trade union and to participate in the union's activities;
(c) every worker has the right to strike;
(d) every employer has the right to form and join an employers' organisation and to participate in the activities of the organisation; and

589. Section 22 of the Constitution.

(e) every trade union, employers' organisation and employer has the right to engage in collective bargaining.[590]

285. All these rights set the tone in relation to the employer and employee relationship and it is very important that they are upheld and protected.

§3. Labour Regulation

I. The History of Labour Law

286. Prior to the discovery of gold and diamonds in South Africa, the economy could by and large be described as agrarian, with the main economic activity being agriculture. The relationship between employers and domestic workers and farm workers was governed by various Acts, including the Master and Servants Act 15 of 1856.[591] At this time, the employment relationship was regarded as being a 'master and servant' relationship.

287. When gold and diamonds were discovered, mining activity in South Africa rapidly increased. The booming mining industry brought with it an influx of labour and workers to the mines. The first South African trade union, the Carpenters' and Joiners' Union, was established in 1881, largely to protect the interests of skilled foreign workers working on the mines.[592]

288. As the mining industry developed, the difference in political power between whites and blacks became entrenched as trade unions, catering largely for white workers, mobilised increasingly on the basis of race. In 1911, the Mines and Works Act was passed which reserved various types of work for white workers only.[593] This era was very turbulent and a number of strikes, with the aim of securing the position of white workers on the mines, took place.

289. After the general strike of 1914, martial law was declared and trade union leaders were deported from South Africa. The 'labour peace' which ensued was short-lived as the circumstances of the mines worsened due to the economic depression, a large foreign debt and the rising costs of living.[594] The mines responded by restructuring. This led to a number of white workers being retrenched, which in turn led to the abolition of the ratio between skilled white workers and unskilled black workers on the mines.[595]

590. Section 22 of the Constitution.
591. Section 1 of Master and Servants Act 15 of 1856.
592. Section 2 of Carpenters and Joiners Union Act 1881.
593. Section 2 of the Mines and Works Act 1911.
594. P. Delius, *The History of Migrant Labour in South Africa (1800–2014)*, 17 SHSA 30 (2017).
595. *Ibid.*, at 17.

290. This situation gave rise to the 1922 strike, one of the watershed moments in South African labour history. The result of this strike was the passing of the Industrial Conciliation Act in 1924.[596] This Act was the direct forefather of the Industrial Conciliation Act of 1956, which was later renamed as the Labour Relations Act (LRA) of 1956. This Act accorded recognition to trade unions representing white workers, while a separate system for black workers was created.[597]

291. In 1948, the National Party came into power, which saw the birth of Afrikaner Nationalism. In 1950, the Suppression of Communism Act was passed which led to the large-scale repression of union activists. The 1950s was a turbulent time in the political history of South Africa. This turbulence led to the amendment of the 1956 Industrial Conciliation Act, in order to ensure tougher controls over black workers.[598]

292. The Wiehahn Commission of Inquiry was established in 1979 to investigate the labour situation in South Africa. The resultant report of the Commission went on to change the face of South African labour relations and labour law. The most consequential recommendation made by the Commission was the extension of freedom of association to cover all persons, irrespective of race or sex. The result was that trade unions representing black workers were now able to make use of the machinery of the LRA of 1956.[599]

293. The period between 1991 and 1994 saw the birth of the new democratic South Africa. In 1994, the Interim Constitution, Act 200 of 1993, came into effect. The Act totally changed the constitutional basis of the South African legal system and it became clear that the LRA of 1956 was not in line with the new constitutional order.

294. In 1994, the Department of Labour appointed a ministerial legal task team to draft new labour legislation and the LRA 66 of 1995 came into effect on 11 November 1996. The Act heralded a new era in South African labour law.[600]

II. The Sources of Labour Law

295. The sources of South African labour law include:

(a) legislation;
(b) judicial precedent (judicial decisions), including arbitration awards;
(c) collective agreements;
(d) common law; and

596. *Ibid.*, at 18.
597. *Ibid.*, at 18.
598. *Ibid.*, at 19.
599. Section 1 of the LRA.
600. *Ibid.*

(e) custom and legal writings.[601]

296. Since the democratisation of South Africa after April 1994, the country's labour law was among the first areas of law to be reformed. The main employment law statutes of South Africa are the following:

(a) the Labour Relations Act 66 of 1995 (LRA);
(b) the Basic Conditions of Employment Act 75 of 1997 (BCEA);
(c) the Employment Equity Act 55 of 1998 (EEA);
(d) the Skills Development Act 97 of 1998 (SDA);
(e) the Unemployment Insurance Act 30 of 1996 (UIA);
(f) the Occupational Health and Safety Act 85 of 1993 (OHSA); and
(g) the Compensation for Occupational Injuries and Diseases Act 130 of 1993 (COIDA).

297. Employment protection legislation applies to all employees who ordinarily work in South Africa. Therefore, the legislation also covers employees who work partly outside South Africa and partly inside South Africa. It also applies regardless of the stated governing law of any employment contract or the nationalities of either the employee or the employer.[602] It is not possible for an employee to contract out of statutory employment protection unless the legislation specifically permits it and only to the extent permissible in terms of the legislation. In many cases, the legislation is supported by codes of practice which may be statutory codes of practice drawn up by the National Economic Development and Labour Council or non-statutory codes of practice issued by the Commission for Conciliation, Mediation & Arbitration (CCMA).[603] These codes of practice, although often merely providing guidelines and accordingly not always being of direct legal effect, are taken into account by the labour courts in deciding whether or not an employer has breached statutory employment regulations. Additionally, there are numerous laws implementing health and safety regulations.

298. Unlike the law in certain other countries, collective agreements are normally legally enforceable between employers and trade unions. The LRA 66 of 1995 ('the LRA') supports the primacy of collective agreements and emphasises the need for organised labour and business to regulate their relationship by entering into collective agreements, which bind the employer, the union's members and, where the union represents more than 50% of the employees in a workplace, and if such intent is stated, non-union members in the workplace.[604]

601. M. Gragon, *Essential Labour Law* 218 (Butterworths, Durban 2016).
602. *Ibid.*, at 218.
603. *Ibid.*, at 219.
604. Section 2 of the LRA.

III. Contract of Employment

299. When discussing the employment contract the starting point should be that a written contract of employment is not strictly a necessary requirement for the validity of an employment relationship.[605]

300. However, the Basic Conditions of Employment Act (BCEA) compels an employer to give an employee a host of prescribed employment details in writing when they start working with that employer.[606] This is to ensure certainty between the employer and employee, and it attempts to protect the 'vulnerable' employee against the employer who holds the purse strings in the event of any disagreement as to the details.

301. It therefore makes more sense to enter into a detailed contract of employment upfront with the employee, and thereby bind him or her to the company's disciplinary codes and the like at the same time, rather than to provide a list of prescribed details in a rather ad hoc or non-contextualised manner. A comprehensive contract also has the benefit of being signed by both parties and is therefore legally binding.[607] The essence of an employment relationship is in the details of its contract regarding commencement, currency and termination since in most cases the document will 'speak for itself'.

IV. Prescribed Written Particulars

302. The contract of employment between the employer and the employee is something that is going to be explored in detail because it is very important to know what is in the contract of employment, for purposes of determining the intention of the parties and the scope of their employment contract.

303. Terms and conditions of a contract of employment are found in section 29 of the BCEA. They are:

(a) *The name and address of the employer* – These may seem like obvious details, but many an employee claim has been thwarted either by insufficient or incorrect details in this regard (e.g., regarding the identity of the employer party, especially in a group or division of companies, and in enforcing a judgment).
(b) *The employee's name* – Again apparently an obvious requirement but it provides certainty as to the parties.
(c) *The employee's occupation or a brief description of the work for which the employee was employed* – Certainty on this issue is required for reasons relating to advancement and remuneration, giving instructions which are reasonable to that post, performance, discipline and the like.

605. Gragon, *supra* n. 602, at 219.
606. Section 10 of the Basic Conditions of Employment Act 75 of 1997.
607. Gragon, *supra* n. 602, at 220.

(d) *The employee's place of work* – If the employee is required or permitted to work at various places, an indication of this. The employee should agree at the outset of the employment relationship that he or she would be required to travel, work at various stations, failing which he or she may not easily be compelled to do so later without an agreement. The employer may have to remunerate the employee additionally for undertaking work at different places, and could not simply compel the employee to do so if it has not been agreed initially in the contract.

(e) *The date of commencement of employment* – This is important for the calculation of benefits such as leave, recognition of length of service and the benefits attached to it – e.g., severance pay in a retrenchment.

(f) *The employee's ordinary work days and work hours* – The BCEA sets minimum standards (more specifically, maximum hours and days that may be worked) in this regard, which may not be changed in most cases even with an employee's consent.

(g) *The employee's wage or the rate and method of calculating wages* – This has undoubtedly been included for certainty, consistency and protection for the employee, in addition to ensuring that the employee is fairly remunerated for leave and for overtime among other things.

(h) *The overtime rate* – It must be clearly communicated.

(i) *Any other payments in cash or kind to which the employee may be entitled (and for payments in kind, the value of those payments)* – Again it is important for calculating the monetary value and benefits to which an employee would be entitled during leave, on termination (e.g., severance pay on retrenchment is calculated at one week's remuneration per completed year of service, not one week's base salary). Remuneration includes the value of a number of benefits.

(j) *The date when remuneration will be paid* – Promotes certainty and consistency.

(k) *Details of any deductions that will be made from the remuneration* – In addition to reasons of certainty, the nature and amount of deductions that can be made from an employee's remuneration is strictly regulated by the BCEA.

(l) *The amounts of leave which can or must be taken* – It will suffice to state that the BCEA strictly regulates when and how much leave may and shall be taken. This relates not only to annual leave but also to sick, maternity and family responsibility leave in respect of which there are legislated minimums that may not be contravened.

(m) *The period of notice* – This too is strictly regulated by the BCEA – the quantity and manner of giving notice of termination of a contract of employment is normally three months, except in exceptional circumstances.

(n) *A description of any bargaining council or sectoral determination that covers the employer's business* – This too is in protection of employee rights since it is often the case that terms and conditions of employment more favourable to the BCEA are collectively negotiated within a bargaining council. The bargaining council standards will then take precedence over those set out in the BCEA.

(o) *Any period of employment with a previous employer that counts towards the employee's period of employment.* For example, the length of service with a seller who transfers its business to the purchaser is obliged to recognise the employee's previous length of service, for the purpose of calculating benefits, such as severance packages, long service awards and the like.

(p) *A list of any other documents that form part of the contract – (and an indication of where a copy of these documents may be obtained).* This would relate to policies and procedures, and the like, of the employer. It again provides certainty to the parties of the employment relationship.[608]

304. If and when any of the above details change, the employee is to be notified of the change and be given a copy of the change by the employer which is in line with fair labour practices of South Africa.

V. Employment Contracts

305. South African labour force has grown and based on this growth and expansion two labour contracts are in existence. Fixed-term contracts, the duration of the contract is clearly specified between the parties. The contract will endure for the specified period, or upon the happening of a particular event or until a particular task is completed.[609] Unless otherwise agreed, such a contract cannot be terminated during its current form without good cause, unless the parties have agreed otherwise. If after the contract has lapsed and the employee remains in the employment of the employer, the contract may be tacitly renewed, provided that it is consistent with the parties' conduct.[610] The LRA expressly provides that non-renewal of a fixed-term contract is equivalent to a dismissal in circumstances where the employee expected the employer to renew it on the same or similar terms but the employer either failed to renew the contract at all or offered to renew it on less-favourable terms.[611]

306. In the case of contract to indefinite period, the duration of the contract is not specified by the parties. The contract will endure until:

(a) it is terminated by agreement;
(b) one of the parties gives the contractually specified or reasonable notice to the other;
(c) either party elects to terminate on fundamental breach;
(d) on retirement of the employee at the agreed age, normally 65 years;
(e) summary termination of the employee;
(f) death of either party; and
(g) insolvency of the employer.[612]

608. Section 29 of the Basic Conditions of Employment Act.
609. Gragon, *supra* n. 602, at 220.
610. *Ibid.*, at 221.
611. Section 186 of the LRA.
612. Gragon, *supra* n. 602, at 221.

VI. Probation

307. It is quite common that employers engage employees for a probationary period, which may be negotiated and stipulated in the contract of employment.[613] After expiry of the probationary period, the employer is entitled to decide whether to retain the services of the employee on a permanent basis. The Code of Good Conduct, contained in the LRA, expressly provides for probationary periods for employees. The Code stipulates that the probationary period must be reasonable given the circumstances of the job and the time it takes to determine the employee's suitability for the job. The probationary period can be extended, in suitable circumstances.[614]

308. The Code also states that following completion of the probationary period, probationary employees should not be dismissed unless they have been given appropriate remedial treatment, and they have been allowed a reasonable period for improvement but have failed to improve their performance. If the employer fails to counsel the probationary employee and thereafter fails to confirm the employee's employment, such termination will amount to a dismissal.[615]

VII. Termination of the Contract of Employment

309. The contract of employment can be terminated on the following grounds in the South African labour market:

(a) on expiration of the agreed period of employment;
(b) on completion of the specified task;
(c) by notice duly given by either party;
(d) by summary termination in the event of a material breach on the part of either party;
(e) by repudiation;
(f) by mutual agreement;
(g) by death of either party;
(h) by the insolvency of the employer; and
(i) by the supervening impossibility of performance, where either party becomes permanently unable to perform his or her obligations in terms of the contract.[616]

310. The contract may not be terminated in the absence of a justified reason.
The LRA expressly recognises the following grounds for termination of the employment contract:

(a) misconduct on the part of the employee;

613. Section 186 of the LRA.
614. Section 187 of the LRA.
615. Section 186 of the LRA.
616. Section 188 of the LRA.

(b) the employee's poor work performance and/or incapacity;
(c) the operational requirements of the employer.[617]

311. The concept of unfair dismissal is a right created by statute and contained in the LRA. Chapter VIII of the LRA, along with an accompanying code of practice, has made a large contribution to systematising and clarifying this important area of South African employment law. Unfair dismissals now fall into four categories:

(a) automatically unfair dismissals;
(b) dismissals which an employer cannot justify on the basis of:
  (i) the employee's conduct;
  (ii) the employee's capacity; or
(c) the operational requirements of the business.[618]

312. Besides these substantive grounds, dismissal will also be unfair where it is not effected in accordance with a fair procedure. Meaning that the procedure followed must be fair and just through giving the concerned employee an opportunity to make the necessary representations and state his or her side of the story.

313. The meaning of dismissal has been extended by statute to include:

(a) a failure to renew a fixed-term contract when there was a reasonable expectation of renewal;
(b) a failure to allow an employee to resume work after maternity leave;
(c) selective employment following a collective dismissal; and
(d) a situation where an employee terminates the contract because the employer has made continued employment intolerable (constructive dismissal).[619]

314. A dismissal will be automatically unfair if it is found to comply with the following grounds:

(a) offends against an employee's rights to freedom of association;
(b) is by reason of an employee's refusal to do protected strikers' work;
(c) is effected to compel an employee to accept a demand relating to employment;
(d) constitutes victimisation for exercising any rights under the statute;
(e) is by reason of an employee's pregnancy; and
(f) constitutes discrimination on some arbitrary ground.[620]

315. An employee's rights emanate from either statute or common law. While there does exist certain residual common law rights arising out of breach of contract which may be proceeded with by an employee to the high court of South

617. Section 188A of the LRA.
618. *Ibid.*
619. *Ibid.*
620. *Ibid.*

Africa, the exercise of these rights is rare and the relevance to liability issues extremely limited. By far the vast majority of cases arise out of a breach of statutory rights and obligations.

316. A dismissal that is not automatically unfair is deemed unfair unless the employer proves that the dismissal is for a fair reason either related to the employee's conduct or capacity or based on the operational requirements of the employer.[621] In addition, the employer must prove that the dismissal was effected in accordance with a fair procedure. Accordingly, even if the dismissal is proven to be related to the employee's conduct, capacity or based on the employer's operational requirements (i.e., substantively fair), it will nevertheless still be unfair (procedurally unfair) if the employer has not followed a fair procedure, as already emphasised above.

§4. Remedies Available

317. An aggrieved employee who has been either dismissed or discriminated against has the following reliefs against the employer. The commissioner may:

(a) order the employer to reinstate the employee from any date not earlier than the date of dismissal;
(b) order the employer to re-employ the employee, either in the work in which the employee was employed before the dismissal or in other reasonably suitable work on any terms and from any date not earlier than the date of dismissal; or
(c) order the employer to pay compensation to the employee.[622]

§5. Conclusion

318. From the above assessment it is clear that the general background of the South African labour market is inclusive and that it aims to put both the employer and the employee on equal footing. This means that equity in the workplace is championed in the interest of ensuring that even employees who find themselves in an uncompromising position are still in a position to claim their rights to fair labour practices. The employer is expected not to abuse his or her position of power but must act in the interests of both the business and the employees, while being guided by the principle of equity and not disregard the rule of law which might yield dangerous results.

621. Section 188 of the LRA.
622. Section 188A of the LRA.

Chapter 2. Religious Ministers and Labour Law

§1. Introduction

319. In this chapter the focus will be on whether religious ministers or pastors qualify as employees in South African labour law. This has been one of the contentious issues in the South African labour market on the basis of the fact that religious ministers owe their allegiance to God and not the church because they are called by God. Furthermore, to interrogate whether religious ministers who conclude contracts of employment with the various churches they serve: does this give rise to the employer and employee relationship, while bearing in mind that ministers are called and are serving God.

320. In South Africa there is uncertainty as to whether religious ministers qualify as employees in terms of the BCEA.[623] Due to this uncertainty various labour legislations and court cases will be discussed to provide clarity and certainty in this matter. Religious ministers play an important role in society in general and their contribution cannot be underestimated because they play a leading role in ensuring that social cohesion is achieved.

§2. The Position of Religious Ministers When it Comes to Employment in South Africa

321. As already discussed in the introduction, in the South African context there is uncertainty when it comes to the employment status of religious ministers. This is attributed to the fact that whether they are employees or not and if so who employs them, is it either the church or God? Various views in the labour market will be discussed with the aim of getting the necessary clarity and position as to the employment status of religious ministers in the South African jurisdiction.

322. Who is an employee in terms of South African labour law? An employee is a person who works under the care and control of an employer in rendering his or her services and in return to be remunerated by the employer for services rendered.[624] As to whether a minister in a church qualifies as an employee is a question that will be discussed below.

323. Although there are no court cases in South Africa in which the church was held vicariously liable for the acts of its priests or ministers, there are judgments in other areas in which the question of whether a minister was an employee or not was decided. For example, in *Schreuder v. NG Kerk Wilgespruit,* the Labour Court found that the minister was an employee of the congregation of the Dutch Reformed

623. Section 2 of the Basic Conditions of Employment Act.
624. *Ibid.*

Church where he worked because a letter of calling (*beroepsbrief*) in which the rights and duties of both parties were set out created a contract of employment.[625]

324. The agreement was that the minister would receive a wage (*traktament*) in exchange for his services to the congregation, which was also regarded as an indication that this was an employment contract.[626] The court also took the provisions of the *Kerkorde*', which *inter alia* contains rules and regulations for the employment of minsters and the termination of their services into account, in church. From the *Kerkorde* it is clear that the minster is regarded as an employee of the church, since it prescribes the requirements for a fair dismissal in terms of the LRA.[627] The court in this case accepted that the minister served more than one employer entity within the church group, namely the congregation, *die ring* and the *synod,* and thus was an employee and all laws in South Africa that deal with the employer and employee relationship were applicable to this contract and the conduct of the church in dismissing the minister was found to amount to breach of contract.[628]

325. In contrast to the *Schreuder* case the Labour Court found in *Church of the Province of Southern Africa, Diocese of Cape Town v. CCMA*, which also dealt with a claim for unfair dismissal, that a priest in the Anglican Church could not be regarded as an employee.[629] The court based its finding on the fact that the parties did not intend concluding an employment contract, and that there was no contract of employment that outlined the terms and conditions between the parties. In a nutshell the court held that the intention of the parties was not clear and thus no contract of employment was in place and the priest in this case did not qualify as an employee.[630]

326. Another interesting judgment to this legal uncertainty with the position of ministers is the court case of *Diocese of Cape Town v. CCMA*. In this case, the court accepted the church's evidence that it only provided the space and opportunity for the priest to fulfil his calling to work for God.[631] The court held that 'the relationship between a church and a minister is not apt, in the absence of clear indications of a contrary intention in the document, to be regulated by a contract of service'.[632] The court emphasised the importance of a contract and it must be clear in the sense that the intentions of the parties must be made known. In a similar vein, in *Salvation Army (South African Territory) v. Minister of Labour*, the court granted a

625. *Schreuder v. NG Kerk Wilgespruit* 1999 20 ILJ 1936 (LC).
626. *Ibid.*
627. *Ibid.*, at 1937.
628. *Ibid.*
629. *Church of the Province of Southern Africa Diocese of Cape Town v. Commission for Conciliation Mediation and Arbitration and Others* (C619/2000) [2001] ZALC 141 (7 September 2001).
630. *Ibid.*
631. *Diocese of Cape Town v. CCMA* 2002 3 SA 385 (LC).
632. *Diocese of Cape Town v. CCMA, supra* n. 1 at 385.

declaratory order to the effect that officers (preachers) of the Salvation Army are not its employees and that the Salvation Army is thus not bound by labour legislation.[633]

327. The court accepted evidence that the Salvation Army only provides the space for the officer to answer his call of duty to God and that the officer is only given guidance on administrative tasks, not on how God is to be served.[634] The fact that no remuneration is paid, but only a living allowance, and that there was no guarantee that this would be paid, also indicated to the court that there was no employment relationship.[635] What is clear from the above is that the stance of the South African courts was that in the light of the perceived special calling of a priest, he will not be regarded as an employee of the church unless it is clear that there was indeed an intention to create such a relationship.[636]

328. Since these judgments were handed down, South African courts have been prepared to hold that even though a contract specifies that it is not an employment contract, the court could, by taking the reality of the relationship into consideration, decide that a contract of employment exists between the parties based on the intention between the parties.

329. Another interesting case to note in the establishment of the relationship between a church and a minister is *Nkosinami Nkomonde v. the Diocese of Pretoria (Anglican Church of Southern Africa).*[637] The issue at the heart of this matter was whether or not priests, elders, ministers and pastors are employees of the church. If they are employees of the church, in whose name do they practice?[638] This issue has come before the CCMA and the Labour Court in various guises with various decisions. As the commissioner wrote in his award. '... an Anglican Priest working at a Diocese and being paid a stipend is performing work and placing his labour potential at the disposal of the Church. His duties are clearly defined, the times at which he must perform certain of his duties are set and he is capable of being performance managed by his seniors.'[639]

330. According to section 200A of the LRA, such a person can be presumed to be an employee. Indeed, the award continues, 'If one approaches the matter from an atheistic point of view then what is left behind is quite obviously an employment relationship.'[640]

---

633. *Salvation Army (South African Territory) v. Minister of Labour* (J 464/02) [2004] ZALC 64 (2 Sep. 2004).
634. *Ibid.*
635. *Salvation Army (South African Territory) v. Minister of Labour, supra* n. 634, at 65.
636. *Ibid.*
637. *Nkosinami Nkomonde v. the Diocese of Pretoria (Anglican Church of Southern Africa)* 2015 4 SA 399 (LC).
638. *Ibid.*
639. *Nkosinami Nkomonde v. the Diocese of Pretoria, supra n. 638, at 400.*
640. *Ibid.*

331. Against this argument the commissioner then writes:

> *I believe it is necessary to consider a fundamental concept of what a Christian Church is and where it allegedly derives its authority from. The Theocratic and hierarchical structure is as follows:*
> *At the top is 'God', then Jesus, then the Angels and then one drops down to the Earthly realm were one has the Church, a hierarchical structure within that particular Church, which cascades down to the Priest at the bottom.*[641] *All structures below God derive their authority, power, wisdom and decision-making ability from God. As such, even the Priest at the bottom end of the hierarchy operates under the power of God's spirit and for God's purposes for the people on earth.*[642]
> *The bottom line is that the Priest works for God (according to the Anglican faith) and that any arrangements, including financial payments are simply assistance by the Church to allow the Priest to fulfil his relationship and 'calling' with God to the fullest extent possible.*[643]

332. The commissioner, then went on to rule that as a consequence the church cannot allow an organisation of the state such as the CCMA to tell it whom it may appoint as priests or who it should or should not address. That's a decision left to God.[644]

333. The commissioner ruled that the applicant, in this matter was a priest of the Anglican Church against his dismissal by the church, fell outside the ambit of the LRA. Therefore, the CCMA did not have the authority to consider the matter. In short only God can determine this matter through those who manage the affairs of the church on behalf of God.[645]

334. South African courts have in recent years progressively extended protection against unfair dismissal to categories of persons not previously regarded as employees. Courts interpreted labour legislation in light of the Constitution to include persons with illegal and invalid contracts, as well as persons who were described as independent contractors. Despite this development, the LAC in *Church of the Universal Kingdom of God v. Myeni* held that the minister of religion could not be regarded as an employee because in the court's view the parties had no intention to create legal relations.[646] This judgment can be criticised on the ground that the court regarded the form of agreement, which described the service of the minister of religion as voluntary, as the only determining factor and did not take the

641. *Ibid.*
642. *Nkosinami Nkomonde v. the Diocese of Pretoria, supra n. 638, at 401.*
643. *Ibid.*
644. *Nkosinami Nkomonde v. the Diocese of Pretoria, supra n. 638, at 402.*
645. *Ibid.*
646. *Universal Church of the Kingdom of God v. Myeni and Others* (DA 3/14) [2015] ZALAC 31; [2015] 9 BLLR 918 (LAC); (2015) 36 ILJ 2832 (LAC).

de facto relationship between the parties, which pointed to an employment relationship, into account.[647] The LAC insisted that there must be a contract for the minister of religion to be regarded as an employee, while the Constitution and the LRA do not require a contract.[648] Reliance on English jurisprudence by the LAC is further not appropriate because of certain peculiarities regarding the history of churches in England, which are not shared by South African churches. The LAC did not take the unequal bargaining position of ministers of religion, nor the relevant constitutional rights of the parties, into account. The spiritual dimension of the minister's service seems to be decisive in the court's decision, although the misconduct was not a spiritual matter falling within the domain of the church's own decision-making powers. This matter should have been dealt with by civil courts since there was no danger of doctrinal entanglement.[649]

§3. CONCLUSION

335. In conclusion, from the discussion above and the reasoning of the courts in the above-mentioned court cases, it is clear that in South African law whether a religious minister qualifies as an employee or not is a question of fact. This means that the intention of the parties must be made clear from the beginning of the relationship in terms of a written contract and the contract of service must state out clearly the rights and responsibilities of the religious minister as well as that of the church as an employer.

336. If there is no form of contract or remuneration as well as the terms of service stated and the religious minister is only awarded an allowance by the church, this means that the religious minister will not be considered an employee because he or she would not fit in the requirements of an employee. In such instances as it was alluded above the church would be considered a body that is used to help the religious minister to realise his or her calling to God, and this will not constitute a contract of employment between the religious minister and the respective church. In a nutshell, this means that for a religious minister to be considered an employee and for the church to be held liable on the basis of all labour regulations in South Africa, which are applicable to all employees, must be fulfilled and upheld.

647. *Ibid.*
648. *Ibid.*, at 2833.
649. *Universal Church of the Kingdom of God v. Myeni and Others*, *supra* n. 647, at 2834.

Chapter 3. Other Church Employees and Labour Law

§1. Introduction

337. The contract of employment between the employer and employee is key to be able to distinguish one as an employee or a volunteer of a particular organisation or church in this particular context. In this chapter, based on the background and arguments that were raised in the previous chapter, it is important to draw a distinction between employees of the church and volunteers of the church who normally render their services for free and will not qualify as employees of the church. The aim in this chapter is to ensure or distinguish if indeed church employees or volunteers are protected by the various labour laws in South Africa and if so to what extent.

338. Furthermore, in most instances the church congregants who are normally old and unemployed would render their services to the church for the betterment and prosperity of that church on a voluntary basis. Will this type of service by the congregants of a particular church amount to a contract of employment, thus giving rise to the employer and employee relationship? This is a question of fact and will be considered in this chapter with the aim of ensuring that people who render their services to the church as either employees or volunteers are protected from any form of abuse. The various employees of the church who play a supporting role in addition to the volunteers of the church will be considered because they qualify as employees in South Africa.

§2. Church Employees in South Africa

339. Churches in South Africa are non-profit organisations and are autonomous in the sense that they are independent bodies, and in most instances, some churches have an administrative and clergy offices.[650] Normally, the clergy office will consist of a minister who can be supported by other clergy officials, such as the Bible woman and a deacon who are normally the people who will assist the minister to execute his or her role in terms of spiritual and evangelical works.[651] Furthermore, in the office of the clergy there are preachers of the word of God and these are lay preachers who also assist the minister with the preaching and other evangelical works which are in connection with the church.[652] The Bible women and deacons are people just like ministers who are called from the higher place to serve in the house of the Lord, and these people are not required to work or get formal employment outside the church. This is the position in the Methodist Church and both the Bible woman and deacon will receive a salary or allowance on a monthly basis and get other employment benefits such as medical aid and provident fund.[653] This

650. Siwa, *supra* n. 268, at 3.
651. *Ibid.*
652. *Ibid.*, at 4.
653. *Ibid.*

means that both a Bible woman and deacon are employees of the church and there is an employment contract between them and the church in the sense that they will report to the relevant church minister, who will also be responsible for allocating work for them in terms of the church operations.[654]

340. Bible women and deacons are also expected to retire at the given time just like ministers and give other people an opportunity to lead the church for the purposes of its sustenance and growth for generations to come.[655] Deacons and Bible women can also be dismissed from their role in cases where it is found that they acted with misconduct and in violation of the rules and procedures of the church.[656] The same could be said of a minister once it has been established that he or she is an employee and is involved in conduct that puts the image of the church into disrepute. In such instances the minister will have to be disciplined and in other instances he or she can be dismissed by the church.[657] From the role and assessment of the position of both the Bible woman and deacon it is clear that they are employees of the church in the office of the clergy, and they are protected by the various labour law provisions in South Africa and in their employment contract such provisions must be incorporated. This means that the church cannot dismiss them unfairly or discriminate against them as this will be contrary to the provisions of labour law and most importantly in violation of the provisions of the Bill of Rights as per section 9 of the Constitution.[658] When it comes to lay preachers this is not the case as these are people who also say that they are called to serve in the house of the Lord and in return for having rendered all the services as per the office of the clergy they do not receive any remuneration or donation.[659] Lay preachers have employment outside the church and for them to be preachers of the word of God is a special gift on its own in the sense that it is not everyone who can be a preacher and for them to execute this role is without a doubt an honour which no money or gratitude can express or equate.[660] From the role of lay preachers in the church it is clear that these are people who are congregants of the church and play an important role in ensuring that the Gospel of God is spread out, and they are not employees of the church. This means that lay preachers are not employees of the church and are not protected by any labour laws in South Africa.[661] Lay preachers hold the view that their reward is not from this earth but it is from a higher place which is in heaven, and that reward awaits them when they leave this earth.[662] From the office of the clergy it is clear that it is not everyone who is in that office qualifies to be an employee as it was outlined above. However, all the participants in that office share a common goal or vision that the word of God must reach the four corners of the world as per their respective callings in the ministry of Christ.

---

654. *Ibid.*, 5.
655. *Ibid.*
656. *Ibid.*, at 6.
657. *Ibid.*
658. Section 9 of the Constitution.
659. Siwa, *supra* n. 268, at 6.
660. *Ibid.*, at 7.
661. *Ibid.*
662. *Ibid.*, at 8.

341. Another arm of operations in churches today in South Africa is the administrative office and in this office the people who work in it play a supporting role to the clergy. The personnel in this office will include the secretary to the minister and other administrative staff. In most cases the secretary and the administrative personnel will work in the office on a full-time basis and be provided with a contract of employment in relation to how they are going to be remunerated and their working conditions.[663] These people will support the clergy and ensure that the church administration is handled with care and efficiency in the interest of the church. Furthermore, the administrative personnel will report to the minister and can also be disciplined by the church in case it is found that there is a violation of the Code of Conduct or such a personnel has acted in an improper manner.[664] Meaning that the administrative personnel in churches are employees and are covered by the labour laws of South Africa against any form of discrimination or unfair dismissals which will be contrary to the interests of the public. However, it is important to also note that the administrative personnel of a church can be volunteers who are also members of that particular church and this will be a different story and position. Meaning that these administrative personnel will not qualify as employees of the church and will not receive any form of labour protection but will be volunteers who have an aim of ensuring that they work towards the development of their church. This form of conduct will be considered as good will, and it will not constitute employment.[665]

342. Furthermore, apart from the office of either the clergy or administrative personnel there are also other office bearers who work in church, including the caretaker and the gardener who are in charge with ensuring that the church premises are kept clean and safe.[666] In most cases the church caretaker and gardener will have an employment contract with the church and do not have to be a church member of that particular church domination. This means that they are only rendering a service to the church which is the upkeep of the church and its premises and to be remunerated for the services rendered.[667] Caretakers and gardeners will normally report to the office of the minister who will act on behalf of the church and ensure that they render their services as per their employment contract.[668] It is possible that in this case some church members of the various dominations can delegate this role to their members due to financial constraints and in such a case there will not be any contract of employment and the services rendered will be a voluntary initiative which aims to benefit the church.[669] In this case there will not be any employment contract in place and both the caretaker and the gardener will not be remunerated because they will be acting in the interest of the church. Under these circumstances the church will provide some kind of a gift or gratitude to the various congregants

663. *Ibid.*
664. *Ibid.*, at 9.
665. *Ibid.*
666. *Ibid.*, at 10.
667. *Ibid.*
668. *Ibid.*, at 11.
669. *Ibid.*

who have rendered their services as required by the church.[670] This gift will not amount to remuneration because it will create an impression that a contract of employment exists between them and the church. When it comes to the employment of church employees, the facts and circumstances of each case need to be taken into account to determine if we are dealing with an employee or volunteer in church because these are two different things.

§3. CONCLUSION

343. To qualify as employees of the church, they need to comply with the provisions of the Labour laws in South Africa and must have an employment contract with the church for the services to be rendered. People who are volunteers in church with the aim of assisting in church and who are thanked for the services do not qualify as employees and cannot claim employment benefits to that effect. In a nutshell the intention of both the church and the various personnel must be made clear when it comes to the obligations they intend to create in order for an employment contract to be created.

670. *Ibid.*, at 12.

Part VII. Religious Communities and Protection of the Individual

344. In this part, the discussion focuses on the protection of fundamental rights which an individual enjoys as a member of a religious or cultural group. However, it is important for the reader to note that some of these fundamental rights which an individual enjoys as a member of a group have been extensively discussed in the text earlier, and it will not be necessary to repeat in this chapter. The fundamental rights which an individual as a member of a religious or cultural community, which have been discussed already, include the right to privacy; freedom of expression; due process norms and the various religious groups, bearing in mind the pluralistic nature of the South African community; and the issue of unfair discrimination both from the constitutional and legislative point of view.

345. The topics that will be covered in this part are the following: freedom to marry; professional secrecy and medical deontology will be discussed under one heading due to the fact that they interrelate and have to do with the employment or profession which a member of a religious community holds in society and lastly there will be a discussion on penal law and religion as the concluding chapter on the topic of the role of an individual in a religious or cultural community.

Chapter 1. Freedom to Marry

§1. Introduction

346. In the new South Africa where the Constitution is the supreme law of the land, it means that people's fundamental rights are entrenched and protected by the Constitution and this includes the freedom of an individual person to marry. An individual of a certain religious group or culture can get married to another person who is from another religious or cultural group, and they can conclude into either a civil marriage, Muslim marriage or an African customary law marriage. This is to affirm and show the diversity of the population of South Africa, and that today black and white people irrespective of their religion or culture can marry each other. It is important to note that this was not the position during the colonial and apartheid era, in which only whites would be married to each other and the same would apply with black people. Mixed racial marriages were not permitted during the apartheid era.

347. However, in the new South Africa the position without a doubt has changed to such an extent that the freedom to marry is left to the individuals to choose as they please irrespective of their religion or cultural background. Despite this wonderful progress in the development of the South African law in recognition and affirmation of the dignity of people to have the freedom to choose who they want to marry, there are challenges. Some of these challenges will be discussed in this chapter with the aim of exposing this hindrance as well as coming up with solutions in the process in order to ensure that the freedom to marry which an individual enjoys is protected and promoted.

§2. Failure to Recognise Religious Marriages

348. South Africa's Constitution allows for laws to be passed that recognise religious and traditional marriages as well as personal laws and family laws. These are systems that regulate marriage, divorce, matters affecting children, including the important aspect of guardianship, custody, access, maintenance and succession as well as inheritance.[671] This is a serious departure from the colonial and apartheid period as already discussed above, when South Africa's common law definition was restrictive in such a way that marriage was defined as a union between one man and one woman. In other words, a legal marriage in South Africa was characterised by heteronormativity and monogamy.[672] This was at the exclusion of same-sex marriages and polygamous marriages and this affected African customary marriages, Muslim marriages, Jewish and Hindu marriages, which are all polygamous in nature and the freedom to marry an individual was compromised.[673]

671. C. Rautenbach, *Gender Equality and Religious Family Laws in South Africa*, 3 Queensland UTLJ 168 (2003).
672. *Ibid.*
673. *Ibid.*, at 169.

349. The situation changed when the Constitution was adopted and, for example, there was an adoption of the Recognition of Customary Marriages Act, which afforded African customary marriages full legal recognition.[674] Furthermore, there was an adoption of the Civil Union Act which made marriages between same-sex couples legal and enforceable in South Africa.[675] These two pieces of legislations aimed to promote the freedom of an individual to marry. without paying attention to his or her religion, culture, gender or sexual orientation which is key in a constitutional democracy.

350. However, the above cannot be said about polygynous marriages such as Muslim marriages, Hindu marriages and Jewish marriages because they have not yet been afforded legal recognition. This failure on the part of the legislature can be said to be tantamount to saying that religious marriages are inferior and less deserving of legal protection and enforcement.[676] Furthermore, this failure infringes the rights to human dignity, freedom of religion and equality of spouses in religious marriages and the children born within those marriages.[677] It can be argued that also this failure restricts the freedom of an individual to exercise their right to choose whom they want to marry, and this cannot be permitted in the new South Africa.

351. Women are particularly badly affected by this non-recognition, for example a Muslim wife who has substantially a small estate compared to her husband. She could be left financially destitute should the marriage end in a divorce.[678] Yet she has no recourse under South African law because her marriage is not legally recognised, but given putative recognition like a civil marriage.[679] Furthermore, Muslim women are also at a disadvantage because polygyny is not regulated. This means that men can enter into subsequent marriages without their knowledge and this is very unfair as well on the basis of equality.[680] Women also have difficulty accessing a Muslim divorce even though their right to divorce is recognised under Islamic law. This has resulted in many women being held hostage in unwanted marriages, which again affects the freedom to marry as protected by the Constitution.[681] This means that people who are married under religious marriages or law are at a serious disadvantage.

352. Government is called upon to give attention to the plight which the Muslim community and other minority religious groups experience, which is without a doubt unjust. The non-recognition of these unions not only is it an infringement to their right to freedom of religion and belief but also it could be taken further to say

674. Section 1 of the Recognition of Customary Marriages Act 120 of 1998.
675. Section 1 of the Civil Union Act.
676. Rautenbach, *supra* n. 672, at 169.
677. Section 10 of the Constitution.
678. F. Cachalia, *The Future of Muslim Law in South Africa*, 12 OP 22 (1991).
679. *Ibid.*
680. *Ibid.*, at 23.
681. *Ibid.*

that it is a violation of the human dignity of the people who are part of these minority religious groups.[682] The freedom to marry, which each and every person enjoys in the Republic, is compromised when it comes to these minority religious groups, and it is unjust because it is not in line with section 36 of the Constitution which is the limitation clause.[683] Furthermore, the non-recognition of Muslim marriages and other minority religions means that people who are members of these religious groups at some point will desist to conclude into such marriages or union. However, it will not be on the basis of their free will but on the fact that they want to avoid the consequences which come with the non-recognition of such unions. This is unfortunate and requires urgent attention of the legislature. Freedom to religion or culture goes hand in hand with the freedom to marry and they speak one and the same thing with the purpose of affirming the independence and autonomy of an individual in the new South Africa.

§3. Conclusion

353. In conclusion, freedom to marry is central in a democratic dispensation and it is something that the government must never underestimate and must ensure that it is protected to avoid the injustices of the past. Government, and in particular the legislature, is called upon to act with the necessary urgency in giving recognition to Muslim marriages and other minority religious marriages, and as it was discussed the failure to do so is in actual fact a direct violation of the freedom to religion and freedom to marry, which are without a doubt central pillars of building social cohesion.

682. Section 10 of the Constitution.
683. Section 36 of the Constitution.

Chapter 2. Professional Secrecy and Medical Deontology

§1. Introduction

354. Members or individuals of either a religious congregation or cultural group apart from their beliefs and values belong to different professions. This means that an individual as a member of a religious or cultural group makes contact with different people or groups as part of his or her employment among other things. What happens if there is a dispute between the profession of an individual and their culture or religion at a particular point in time. This conflict of interests will be explored in this chapter.

355. Professional secrecy and medical deontology are discussed in this chapter as one because they both have to do with a professional life of a member of a religious or cultural group. Due to this connection between the two, they will be discussed in this chapter together with the aim of showing or drawing a distinction between a religious life of an individual and the professional life of that particular individual. Furthermore, it will be explored as to how a balance could be maintained between the professional life and a religious life of an individual, to avoid the conflict between the two as mentioned.

§2. Professional Secrecy

356. As already outlined above members of a religious or cultural group can occupy very high positions or professions based on their level of education or talents. It is important to note that freedom of trade or occupation is guaranteed in South Africa by the Constitution and this includes members of religious and cultural dominations.[684] This means that religious and cultural organisations have individuals in the church who are qualified as lawyers, accountants, medical doctors, nurses and teachers to name but a few. The professions that are listed above and those which are not mentioned have their professional standards and procedures, which an individual irrespective of his or her religion or culture must comply with in order to be admitted to that profession. For example, if an individual church member is admitted as an attorney in South Africa it means that all of his or her professional conduct will be tested and regulated by the law society of that particular area and will be expected to take an oath.[685] Taking an oath is ensuring that individual attorneys are to uphold and protect their profession and that they will owe their allegiance to the profession they have chosen. This will mean that the individual concerned is expected to protect and uphold the integrity of that profession, irrespective of his or her religious beliefs or convictions.[686]

684. Section 22 of the Constitution.
685. Section 11 the Attorney's Act.
686. Section 12 the Attorney's Act.

357. This means that they are expected to act in the interest of their profession based on the work they do, and in most instances it will be in the public interest to act in that particular manner, and hence the religious or cultural convictions of that particular individual will take a back seat or be limited, and it will be justified.[687] In cases where the individual professional decides to act contrary to the prescribed procedures and rules of his or her profession – which in this case as an attorney with the aim of promoting and protecting his or her religious or cultural beliefs – it can lead to a disciplinary hearing and dismissal of that particular individual on the basis that he or she has disregarded his or her oath of office, which constitutes gross negligence.

358. Furthermore, an individual member of a religious or cultural group must be in a position to draw a distinction between his or her professional life and his or her religious life. This is very much fundamental because a religious or cultural life of an individual is subjective in nature and based on principles of love, caring and compassion and while the professional life is the exact opposite. Professional life is an objective process in which no feelings are applicable but only the correct interpretations and applications of the laws and standards are supreme.[688] Maintaining and drawing a distinction between the professional and religious or cultural life of an individual is key because the two are different and must be kept separate in most instances to avoid conflict because in most instances an individual might be conflicted between his or her professional life and their religion or culture.

359. Drawing a distinction between professional life and religious or cultural life of an individual will help the particular professional to maintain professional privilege and this means that communication between that professional and his or her clients is privileged.[689] Meaning that a professional is prevented to disclose communication he or she had with clients to anyone, and the courts cannot compel the said professional to disclose such information because it will be based on the fact that it is privileged and must be protected.[690] If that professional discloses the said information it will result in dire consequences for the said professional in the sense that he or she can be dismissed for breaching this privileged information and in some instances clients can institute a civil claim against the said professional for the violation of their right to privacy based on the unwarranted disclosure.[691] This means that individual professionals must exercise the necessary caution and ensure that privileged information that emanates from their professional capacity is not disclosed in their private or religious spaces, even though such information adversely affects their private or religious life.

687. Section 36 of the Constitution.
688. Section 2 of the Attorney's Act.
689. Section 20 of the Attorney's Act.
690. Section 21 of the Attorney's Act.
691. Section 25 the Attorney's Act.

§3. MEDICAL DEONTOLOGY

360. Medical deontology has to do with an aspect of maximum professionalism that is expected on the part of a medical doctor in ensuring that the patient is treated successfully.[692] A great deal of professional ethics is expected of a medical doctor who in this case can also be a member of a religious or cultural group, and the medical practitioner must act in the best way possible as prescribed by their profession in treating the patient.[693] This will entail giving the patient the prescribed medication, maintaining the diagnosis and treatment of the patient private and avoid making conversations that will endanger the health and well-being of that particular patient.[694] In a nutshell a medical practitioner is expected to provide a great deal of support and professionalism and act ethically in the process because there is a thin line between religion and ethics, but in this instance the medical doctor is bound by the ethics of the profession and not that of his or her religious convictions.[695]

361. In cases where it is found that a medical doctor has acted contrary to his or her oath of office and followed his or her conscience, which can have a religious or cultural component, the medical practitioner will be subjected to disciplinary proceedings by the regulatory body which is the Health Professions Council of South Africa (HPCSA). In some instances he or she will be suspended or dismissed from practising medicine.[696] This is because the HPCSA acts as a watchdog against medical practitioners who abuse their position against vulnerable members of the community.

§4. CONCLUSION

362. From the above it is very much clear that professionalism is key in maintaining a working balance between religion and professional life. These two roles must not be mixed because if they do then a conflict will arise and it will be without a doubt to the disadvantage of the individual member of that religious domination or cultural group. Furthermore, religious and cultural groups must encourage their members to pursue various career opportunities, which in return will strengthen and boost their existence as well as sustenance on the basis of the support which these professionals will bring to the church. Furthermore, it will be argued in the chapter to come that direct financing of religious organisations or communities depends on active members of that particular religion or culture taking part in active economic opportunities.

---

692. Section 26(1) the Attorney's Act.
693. W. Mary, *Medical Ethics Made Easy*, 21 Professional Care Management 81 (2016).
694. *Ibid.*, at 22.
695. *Ibid.*, at 23.
696. *HPCSA Regulatory Body of South Africa's Medical Practitioners*, https://citizen.co.za/news/south-africa/1991655/health-professions-council-struggles-in-fight-against-corruption/ (accessed 17 Aug. 2018).

Chapter 3. Penal Law and Religion

§1. Introduction

363. South Africa is a young democracy under the rule and supremacy of the Constitution, which took over the role from parliament which used to pass arbitrary laws to the detriment of the majority of black people. Despite the infancy, South African Constitution has made great strides in the protection of fundamental rights which all the people of South Africa enjoy today. However, the same cannot be said about religion and culture in South Africa because they are ancient and form part and parcel of the daily lives of the people of South Africa and the broader continent of Africa.

364. This chapter will look into areas where the religious and cultural beliefs of people are compromised or violated by others. If indeed it is found that there is such a violation of either religion or culture what would be the mitigating factor to address the injustice in terms of the law. While bearing in mind that freedom of religion and culture is firmly protected by the Constitution and if there is a threat to this particular right then the law must provide the necessary remedies to address this injustice.

§2. Penal Law and Religion

365. Throughout this research project, the importance of the role of religion and culture in South Africa is emphasised, and it can be said that they both form part and parcel of the lives of all people in the Republic. In addition, remembering the role religion played in the liberation of South Africa during the dark era of apartheid and how currently in the new democratic dispensation religion plays a major role in bringing the necessary social cohesion.[697] This significant and important role that is played by religion on the daily lives of the people of South Africa is the major reason why today freedom of religion and culture is one of the fundamental rights in the Constitution.[698] This affirms and recognises the role religion has played and is still playing to this very day, which is something that cannot be underestimated without a doubt. The fact that religion is fully protected by the Constitution and other pieces of legislation means that it is significant in society and any threat to this freedom to religion will amount to a threat to the Constitution. Freedom of religion and culture means the liberty to choose without any fear or favour, and this must be done in a way that does not undermine or discriminate against the religion or culture of other people.[699] This means that freedom of expression in connection with a religion or culture does not mean that it is a freedom to promote one religion

697. J.C.W. Van Rooyen, *Dignity, Religion and Freedom of Expression in South Africa*, 12 OR 1 (2011).
698. Section 15(1) of the Constitution.
699. Van Rooyen, *supra* n. 698, at 2.

or culture at the expense of the other.[700] Freedom of expression in this case means the freedom to exercise and enjoy your cultural and religious practices in line with the rule of law.

366. South Africa being a pluralistic society, diversity is the order of the day and must be embraced. This means that the majority religious dominations cannot discriminate or dominate the minority, but all religious or cultural groups must coexist and the element of equality and fairness must be present in this particular space.[701] Furthermore, this means that hate speech, which is directed at destroying the image and reputation of one religion by the other, is not condoned in South Africa, and it will be contrary to the provisions of freedom of expression.[702] Hate speech or slander also violates fundamental rights which include in particular human dignity and freedom of religion, and this can result in the guilty party being held liable for damages by a civil court.[703] Furthermore, hate speech can in some cases lead to criminal prosecution because it can result in people engaging in violent activities in some instances with the aim of protecting their religious or cultural belief.[704] This shows that when there are cases of hate speech among different religions or cultural groups, it is important to resort to law-enforcement agencies first because failure to do so can result in people taking the law into their own hands, resulting in severe consequences.

367. Law as a regulatory mechanism, in this case the Constitution as the supreme law, must intervene and ensure that all religious and cultural organisations are protected and maintained. There must not be any form of bias or favouring one at the expense of the other, but the rule of law must be the dominating one all the time. Furthermore, law has indeed a role to play as a mediator in cases where religious and cultural organisations are at loggerheads with each other and bring the necessary stability and order, with the aim of ensuring that the rule of law remains supreme all the time. The role of the law as a mediator is key in order to prevent and stop religious wars from taking place in the Republic, which is unfortunately the order of the day in some African countries.

§3. CONCLUSION

368. Tolerance and respect for the rule of law and other religious and cultural groups is expected from each and every member of South Africa with the aim of ensuring the democracy of South Africa is protected and upheld at all costs. Failure to respect the religious and cultural affiliations of other people will result in dire consequences, which can either lead to a civil or a criminal claim in the process. This must be avoided at all costs and a great deal of tolerance for diversity is key

700. Section 16(1) of the Constitution.
701. Van Rooyen, *supra* n. 698, at 3.
702. Section 16(1) of the Constitution.
703. Van Rooyen, *supra* n. 698, at 4.
704. *Ibid.*, at 5.

in ensuring that different religious and cultural dominations coexist in South Africa because they all play an important role in the building of the new South Africa.

Part VIII. Church Financing

Chapter 1. Direct and Indirect Financing of Religious Communities

§1. Introduction

369. Religious communities for their survival and continuous existence need the necessary financial support from within the religious community and also from external people or donors. This must be done within the parameters of the law of the Republic and there must not be any form of criminality during this process of raising funds.

370. Religious communities like any autonomous institutions have needs and obligations to fulfil and raising funds is one of the major factors that contribute towards the existence of that religious community or organisation. This is one of the major reasons that religious organisations are not required to pay tax in South Africa, unlike other countries such as Germany and Denmark.[705] It can be said that the reason why religious communities or organisations are not taxed in South Africa is because of the rich history and role religion has played in the democratic dispensation of South Africa, and furthermore not to put financial burden on them which can adversely affect their existence. This chapter will focus on how religious communities receive or raise funds directly or indirectly with the sole purpose of keeping their ministry alive in their respective communities and also in the interest of their members.

§2. Direct Financing of Religious Communities

371. Section 11 of the South African Charter of Religious Rights and Freedom states that like all voluntary associations, a religious institution has the right to perform different actions to further its objectives and to receive, manage and spend money for that purpose.[706] During this initiative, religious institutions are expected to act as responsible bodies to govern themselves in financially sound and responsible ways and to act in the best interests of their members.[707] Direct financing

705. M. Valova, *Financing Churches and Religious Societies in the 21st Century*, 322 RCVP 146 (2010).
706. Section 11 of the South African Charter of Religious Rights and Freedom.
707. *Ibid.*

entails a process in which within the members of that particular religious community or institution different fund-raising initiatives are made in order to keep the ministry going. Direct financing of religious institutions can include members taking the initiatives by paying their offerings monthly to the church; by contributing to church collections; by paying their affiliation or registration fees annually; by participating in thanksgiving services, which is normally annual.[708] These are some of the recognised fundamental practices which are directly contributing to the financial position of a religious community. This is one of the ways in which members of that particular religious community or institution are taking charge in building as well as preserving their religious community by ensuring that it is financially sound to meet its obligations either on a monthly or daily basis.

372. Furthermore, direct financing from the members of the religious community or organisation can emanate from engaging in different fund-raising initiatives with the aim of ensuring that the religious ministry is financially afloat and sound. This can include to make talents by inviting other churches to their church and raise funds and while at the same time building relations with other religious groups.[709] Organising choir competitions, concerts and sell tickets to members of that church community and the broader community. During the concert different beverages can be sold to the people who are coming for the concert and this will in the process raise the necessary funds that are required by the church.[710] Direct financing is a way of showing commitment by the members of that religious community to their ministry, and they are expected to lead by example and preserve the ministry for the next generation. Furthermore, direct financing can be seen as a way in which the children of God are showing and expressing gratitude to God for all the blessings and mercies he has showed them.[711] In a nutshell, direct financing of a religious community or organisation can be described as a covenant the children of God have with their Creator and is something that is fundamental. All the funds that are raised either directly or indirectly as will be discussed below must be directed towards the ministry of God in that particular religious community or organisation. In cases where this is not the case, then in most instances the people who are involved with church administration which include the minister can be charged and convicted for fraud and corruption by the law-enforcement agencies in South Africa.[712] This affirms that despite the autonomy of a religious community or organisation it is still subject to the rule of law and must not act contrary to the law.

373. Religious communities or organisations must account for their financial position to their members monthly and annually. This will affirm that it is transparent and ensure that it records as well as audits their financial statements in order to give confidence to their members who are its direct funders for its existence.[713] Furthermore, in South Africa religious communities or organisations are expected to

708. Siwa, *supra* n. 268, at 85.
709. *Ibid.*, at 86.
710. *Ibid.*
711. Holy Bible 2 Corinthians Ch 9: Verses 7.
712. Section 12 of the South African Charter of Religious Rights and Freedom.
713. Siwa, *supra* n. 268, at 87.

submit their financial statements to the South African Revenue Services annually even though they are tax exempted and this is to guard against money laundering and other criminality which can take place in religious communities or organisations.[714] The primary funders of a religious community or organisation are its members, and this gives rise to direct financing of that particular ministry and hence religious communities or organisations are all the time in need of more members with the sole aim of growing their ministry and funding among other things.

§3. Indirect Financing of a Religious Community

374. Indirect financing of a religious community is the opposite of direct financing. Indirect financing has to do with sourcing out funds from external people or businesses who are not part of that religious community or organisation, but must share the same goal in most instances.[715] Indirect financing of a religious community in most cases has to do with the church leadership engaging with sponsors to support the various initiatives or projects of that particular religious community or organisation. This can include looking for sponsors from the local business people; political parties and in some instances to international bodies for funding.[716] In return the sponsors can ask the religious organisation or community to account as to how they utilised the funds and in some instances particularly businesses can request the religious community or organisation to advertise its services to their members in return to the sponsorship they have given them.[717] This will be a reciprocal relationship in which both parties are benefiting from each other, while at the same time building the necessary social cohesion and stability.

375. When it comes to indirect financing of religious communities or organisations it is important to note that an external body must not compel or make a religious community or organisation to compromise its values and the rule of law, to such an extent that it is now seen to promote some form of criminality which is contrary to the law. For example, a religious community or organisation to be used to safe keep proceeds of illegal activity in return for the donation it received will be contrary to the rule of law.[718] Furthermore, religious communities or organisations cannot accept a donation from a business or political party on condition that it is to defame or discriminate against other religious communities or organisations, as this type of conduct will be seen as contrary to public policy and destroying social cohesion.

376. From the above assessment of indirect financing of religious communities or organisations it is clear that for this to happen in order to sustain the ministry of the church it must be a reciprocal relationship based on sound legal principles. This

714. Section 13 of the South African Charter of Religious Rights and Freedom.
715. Valova, *supra* n. 706, at 147.
716. Siwa, *supra* n. 268, at 88.
717. *Ibid.*, at 89.
718. Section 13 of the South African Charter of Religious Rights and Freedom.

means that donors of that religious community or organisation must not impose conditions that will compromise the values and ethos of that religious community, which can result in an act of crime being committed in the process. Religious communities or organisations must not compromise their values in return for donations because if they do then it will be to their detriment and downfall in the process. Religious communities or organisations as important bodies in societies are vehicles of social cohesion and nation building, and they must uphold the rule of law and their values or morality even if it means that they are not to receive external donations or funding.

§4. Conclusion

377. In conclusion, from the discussion above it is very much clear that church funding either direct or indirect is fundamental for the continuous existence of a religious community or organisation. However, this does not mean that religious communities or organisations can engage in illegal activities to obtain church funding but are bound by their internal processes as well as the rule of law in South Africa which sets and guides them in relation to how they are expected to get funding. In cases where they are found to act contrary to those processes and laws they will face the full might of the law, which can put their existence in serious risk or threat, if necessary care is not exercised.

Part IX. Education

Chapter 1. Religious Education in Public and Private Schools

§1. Introduction

378. In this chapter emphasis will be placed on the education system of South Africa with specific reference to religious education included in the school curriculum. South African education system just like that of other countries in the world is divided into two parts or sections, that is, public and private schools. This is similar to the public and private healthcare sectors in South Africa which was discussed in the earlier chapter, when emphasising recognised fundamental rights. A discussion will be drawn in this particular instance as to how both private and public schools operate in South Africa in fulfilling their constitutional obligations of giving adequate access to education as per the Constitution.[719]

379. Furthermore, section 7 of the South African Charter of Religious Rights and Freedom states that everyone has the right to be educated or to educate their children or to have them educated in accordance with their religious or philosophical convictions.[720] This means parents have the right to choose the form of education for their children and schools are delegated the parental authority when they take on the task of education, because the state has no prior right to educate the young especially on religious matters which is something people will exercise independently and freely without the interference of the state.[721]

§2. Religious Education in Public Schools

380. Public schools in South Africa are considered to be in a position similar to the public hospitals as discussed above, because this system of education is faced with lots of challenges which include lack of resources; poor infrastructure; fewer committed teachers and overcrowding in most instances.[722] It is stated in the South

719. Section 29(1) of the Constitution states that everyone has a right to a basic education, including adult basic education, and to further education, which the state through reasonable measures must make progressively available and accessible.
720. Section 7(1) of the South African Charter of Religious Rights and Freedom.
721. Section 15(1) of the Constitution.
722. *Education in South Africa a System in Crisis*, https://city-press.news24.com/News/education-in-south-africa-a-system-in-crisis-20160531 (accessed 19 Oct. 2018).

African Constitution that each and every one or child in this instance has a right to access to quality education.[723] This means that public schools are the ones that are fulfilling this particular role for the people of South Africa, and most if not all public schools are no-fee schools. This simply means that they are fully funded by the government.[724] Public schools apart from offering mainstream educational curriculum to the children, for example subjects like Mathematics, English, and Biology to name but a few, they also offer religious education, for example Biblical studies.[725] Furthermore, each and every morning in most if not all public schools children are expected to gather at the school hall or ground for their daily prayers and for the school announcements and this is one practice that forms part and parcel of religious education in public schools.[726]

381. Public schools are playing a very vital role when it comes to the education system of all the children of South Africa, and they must be supported and protected to ensure that they are sustained. Freedom of religion includes the principle that every person has the right to receive and provide religious education, training and instruction, even in public schools.[727] As in all education, the state may choose to subsidise this education, which is the case in public schools by even inviting church ministers to come and minister to the children who belong to a certain religious belief about the importance of that religion or belief.[728] This is another example of the approach in South Africa in which the government is not prohibited to be involved in religious matters, but it has a positive duty to promote and facilitate the exercise of the right to religious freedom as provided by the Constitution.[729] The only condition that is imposed is when the state does engage with religion, for example to subsidise religious education and training, it has to act impartially and may not favour anyone or discriminate against anyone. This will entail the government to consult with all religions in that particular area or community to ensure credibility of programmes and to minimise any fears from religious communities.[730] This means that care should also be given to the principles of accommodation and alternative delivery so that diverse means are not confused with the ends the state wishes to achieve.

382. People and children in particular carry their convictions with them, also in public places like schools, and must be offered an opportunity and space to observe their religion. Logically, this means ethos will reflect the beliefs or convictions of the majority in the school. However, this ethos must be practised in an equitable, free, voluntary and non-discriminatory way. The rights of minorities must be respected and no one in school may be victimised or discriminated against because

723. *Ibid.*
724. *Ibid.*
725. *Ibid.*
726. Section 15(1) of the Constitution.
727. Section 29(1) of the Constitution.
728. Section 7(2) of the South African Charter of Religious Rights and Freedom.
729. Section 7(1) of the South African Charter of Religious Rights and Freedom.
730. Section 7(2) of the South African Charter of Religious Rights and Freedom.

their beliefs or convictions differ from those of the majority.[731] The law challenges public schools to develop mechanisms and processes to ensure that these conditions are met, with the aim of ensuring that children from different religious backgrounds are accommodated and not discriminated against on the basis of their religion. This means that public schools must embrace the diversity of the South African community and not see it as an excuse to favour one group at the expense of the other.

§3. Religious Education in Private Schools

383. Private schools are accessed by children whose parents are able to access this form of education in South Africa, which is independent education from the state. Private education is normally considered to be superior to the public education system because of adequate resources; limited number of children and committed educators as well as good infrastructure as compared to the public education system.[732] Children who access private education just like their peers in public schools in addition to their mainstream educational curriculum they are also offered religious studies and they will also have their morning or afternoon devotions to enable them to stay in touch with their religious convictions even if they are in school.[733] Furthermore, parents will choose to educate their children in a private school that will promote, or is closely linked with, their religious beliefs or convictions. Section 7(3) of the South African Charter of Religious Rights and Freedoms states the right to establish private educational institutions on the basis of a particular religion or philosophy or faith, and the right to observe and impact religious convictions.[734] Such a private institution may refuse to promote, teach or practice other beliefs or convictions. Parents apply to and contract with such an institution on a voluntary basis and it should be accepted that they cannot then object on behalf of their children to the religious activities of the institution.[735]

384. To allow an objector to change a school effectively subordinates religious rights in association with individual rights. The right to exit exists, and it is preferable as a last resort should accommodation become impractical or impossible.[736] There is no right to obliterate the belief frameworks of a single ethos school because a learner may object to the religious or philosophical viewpoint of a school. It is viewed that the alternative approaches that misapply appropriate accommodation as a misunderstanding of how the principles of reconciling different beliefs should operate properly alongside respect for diversity and accommodation.[737]

731. *Ibid.*
732. *Why Private Schools Are an Excellent Investment Opportunity in South Africa*, https://businesstech.co.za/news/business/189369/why-private-schools-are-an-excellent-investment-opportunity-in-sa/ (accessed 19 Oct. 2018).
733. *Ibid.*
734. Section 7(3) of the South African Charter of Religious Rights and Freedom.
735. *Ibid.*
736. Section 7(4) of the South African Charter of Religious Rights and Freedom.
737. *Ibid.*

385. Parents who take their children to private schools to access private education and religious education are bound by the code or practices of that private school, and they must ensure that they comply with them. This means that parents and their children who have subscribed to those rules and practices of the private school voluntarily without any undue influence or pressure are expected to uphold those rules and procedures at all costs. They cannot impose new rules or procedures in the name of religion, unless of course it is found that the code or laws that are in place in that private school are discriminatory in nature or promote violence. Then in such cases they will be declared to be null and void.[738] If this is not the case then the parents or the child involved can elect either to uphold those rules or to exit the school because they have joined the school on a voluntary basis and without undue pressure.

§4. Conclusion

386. It is clear that both private and public education in South Africa are offered in two different environments, but when it comes to religious education both systems aim to ensure that children are educated based on their religious convictions in that particular school without imposing or discriminating against other religious dominations. Furthermore, both private and public schools in their administration of religious education promote diversity and cannot promote propaganda and violence among other things because this will be viewed as contrary to the Constitution which is the supreme law of the land. Based on this assessment it can thus be said that both public and private schools when it comes to religious education share a common goal of using religion as a mechanism to tolerate diversity and to bring the necessary social cohesion to the South African community.

738. Section 7(5) of the South African Charter of Religious Rights and Freedom.

Chapter 2. Religious Schools

§1. Introduction

387. The rich history and foundation of religion in the South African community is something that has been stressed and outlined throughout this book. This means that religion is something that cannot be underestimated in South Africa and that is why it is firmly entrenched and protected by the Constitution. Religion due to its history and position in South Africa and across the globe is a system that has grown and it is now independent from law and political inference but is still subject to the rule of law in South Africa, which is the Constitution.

388. Religion as an independent system is a specialised area of expertise for people who are followers of that religion and those who show interest in that religion. This means that religion apart from serving as a faith to those people who follow it, it has also become a career or a field of study to other people. Due to this development in religion and the pluralistic society of South Africa a need has arisen for the establishment of religious schools with the aim of teaching the theological perspective and understanding of religion or faith. Various religious schools have been established which aim to serve as training institutions for the various religious groups in South Africa, in their diversity.

§2. Religious Schools in South Africa

389. Religious schools which are also called parochial schools or sectarian schools are schools that are aimed at teaching the religious viewpoints of a particular faith or religion.[739] The pluralistic nature of South Africa and the recognition of the different religious beliefs has resulted in different religious schools being developed as well as preserved as one of the ways to ensure that religion or belief remains relevant and in existence in South Africa.[740] The majority of the population of South Africa are Christians as already outlined and this has resulted in the development of Christian religious schools, for example Methodist Church Religious School of South Africa and the Presbyterian Religious School of South Africa, among others.[741] These Christian religious schools teach the Christian doctrines of their respective churches and also cater as training grounds for up and coming prospective ministers and lay preachers of that particular church.[742] Furthermore, in addition to their teaching of a specific indoctrination of a certain church the candidates in these seminary schools are also taught aspects of church administration, and how they are expected to carry themselves in society as well as within the church.[743] This

739. F.T. Hodgson, *Religion and Culture in Public Education in South Africa* 184 (BEHB Printers 2010).
740. *Ibid.*, at 185.
741. Siwa, *supra* n. 268, at 99.
742. *Ibid.*
743. *Ibid.*, at 100.

in a certain way can be seen as a way of preserving the religion or religious convictions because the candidates in these seminary schools are taught the doctrine of the church which can include aspects of history, procedure and processes of the church and the social position of the church. It is something that must be preserved and applied after they qualify.[744]

390. Candidates in seminary schools can spend about three to four years doing their diploma and after this period serve about two to three years of probation before being ordained as ministers.[745] However, this is different from preachers and other candidates like deacons who will be ordained after two years of completing either a certificate or diploma in that particular domination.[746] Furthermore, the people who train these candidates in these seminary schools will be ministers of that particular religious domination, and they must have served for a long time in the church and have the necessary experience and knowledge to impart to the young ones who are in seminary school.[747] Seminary schools in offering religious education are still expected to comply with the rule of law in such a way that they cannot discriminate against other people in need of that type of education or to promote things like violence or propaganda against another religion or group.[748] If this is found to be the case then such a seminary school will be either suspended or closed because it will be promoting illegality which is not in the public interest.

391. Other religious groups which are the minority religious dominations like the Muslim and Jewish also have their religious schools that are in operation in South Africa.[749] Just like the Christian faith or religion, the Muslim; Hindu and Jewish religious schools are teaching the Muslim, Hindu and the Jewish doctrine to its candidates. Normally the people who will be attending these religious schools will either be a leader in that domination or a member with the aim of ensuring that they have a better understanding about their religion or faith.[750] The same standards and procedures that are found in Christian religious seminaries are applicable to the Muslim, Hindu and Jewish religious schools, that is promoting peace and reconciliation without pushing for violence and discrimination. Because engaging in such conducts or practices will be found to be contrary to the Constitution and the rule of law.[751]

392. In the context of African customary law as a religious and cultural practice of the indigenous people of South Africa there is a religious school as well for the people who practice this system.[752] However, not everyone can go to this religious school which is called an initiation school, but only an individual who has a special

744. *Ibid.*
745. *Ibid.* at 101.
746. *Ibid.*
747. *Ibid.*, at 102.
748. Section 2 of the Constitution.
749. Siwa, *supra* n. 268, at 99.
750. Hugh, *supra* n. 211, at 70.
751. *Ibid.*, at 71.
752. Mndende, *supra* n. 84, at 50.

gift of seeing things of the future and who has been chosen by the ancestors for this type of training.[753] The individual chosen to go for an initiation training will be a traditional healer after having gone through an extensive training of about six to twelve months, learning the African way of life as well as how to heal people using different African ways and herbs.[754] Initiation schools for traditional healers are also seen as one of the mechanisms for the preservation of African customary law and practices, and it is a very important and significant process. Initiation schools are also bound by the rule of law and must comply with the law at all costs and not promote any form of illegality or discrimination in their training and practice.

§3. CONCLUSION

393. Religious schools are important for the survival of the various religious dominations in South Africa because they are the foundation for preparing the next generation of people in a particular religious domination. The teachings of these religious schools must be in line with the purpose and supremacy of the Constitution, in such a way that they must not promote discrimination or violence against each other or members of other religious dominations. If this is found to be the case, then freedom of religion and culture will be compromised and there will be some form of consequences in place as laid down by the law.

753. *Ibid.*, at 51.
754. *Ibid.*, at 52.

Selected Bibliography

Articles

Adewole, I.F. 'Challenges and Opportunities in Cancer Control in Africa: A Perspective from the African Organisation for Research and Training in Cancer'. Series 14 (2013): 147.

Akazili, J. & J. Ataguba. 'Health Care Financing in South Africa: Moving Towards Universal Coverage'. CEM 28 (2010): 75.

Baderin, S. 'From International Law of Christianity to the International Law of the Global Citizen'. JHIL 3 (2001): 183.

Beck, S. 'Health Policy, Health Services, and Cancer Pain Management in the New South Africa'. JPSM 17 (1999): 17.

Birdsall, A. *The International Criminal Tribunal for the Former Yugoslavia–Towards a More Just Order?* PCD 8 (2006): 3.

Buscher, B. 'The Political Economy of Africa's Natural Resources and the Great Financial Crisis'. TESG 26 (2011): 137.

Burchell, J.M. 'Media Freedom of Expression Scores as Strict Liability Receives the Red Card: *National Media Ltd v. Bogoshi*'. SALJ 8 (1999): 1.

Cachalia, F. 'The Future of Muslim Law in South Africa'. OP 12 (1991): 22.

Chersich, M. 'Inequalities in Access to Health Care in South Africa'. JPHP 32 (2011): 3.

Chipkin, I. and A. Leatt. 'Religion and Revival in Post-apartheid South Africa'. RESA 9 (2009): 39.

Coertzen, P. 'Constitution, Charter and Religions in South Africa'. AHRLJ 14 (2014): 127.

Delius, P. 'The History of Migrant Labour in South Africa (1800–2014)'. SHSA 17 (2017): 30.

Denny, L., L. Kuhn & P. Batra. 'Utilisation and Outcomes of Cervical Cancer Prevention Services Among HIV-Infected Women in Cape Town'. SAMJ 100 (2010): 39.

De Lille, P. 'The Western Cape Government: History and Regional Development Profile for the City of Cape Town'. WCG 3 (2018): 14.

Evans, D. 'Religion and International Law: Friends or Foes?'. SOAS 32 (2010): 638.

Express, C. 'More Services Needed to Fight Cancer'. UFS 23 (2008): 8.

Falkson, G. & S. Beck. 'Prevalence and Management of Cancer Pain in South Africa'. *Pain* 94 (2001): 76.

Fourie, C. 'Why Is Johannesburg the Economic Hub of South Africa: A City of Opportunities for Entrepreneurs'. *Randburg Sun* 3 (2017): 4.

Foley, H.E. 'Incorporation, Multiple Incorporation and the Conflict of Laws'. *Harvard Law Review* 42 (2000): 516.

Hugh, F.A. 'South African Jews and Apartheid'. *Patterns of Prejudice* 34 (2000): 23.

Jessup, P. 'Transnational Law'. IGLP 8 (2012): 1.

Kauuova, W.R. 'The Religions of Southern Africa: A Synopsis of Their Basic Beliefs'. *Institute for Reformed Studies* 325 (1997): 3.

Kiernan, J. 'African Traditional Religions in South Africa'. *De Jure* 15 (2008): 27.

Lyratzopoulos. G., G. Abel & C. Saunders. 'What Explains Worse Patient Experience in London? Evidence from Secondary Analysis of the Persons Living with Cancer Experience Survey'. BMJ OPEN 4 (2014): 1.

Ma, K. 'Control and Conscience: Positivist Approaches to Religion in India and South Africa'. SOAS LJ 260 (2015): 261.

Mary, W. 'Medical Ethics Made Easy'. *Professional Care Management* 21 (2016): 81.

Marrison, J. 'Nelson Mandela, South Africa's First Black President, Dies at the Age of 95'. *The Washington Times* 5 (2015): 14.

Masuku, T. 'Prophetic Mission of Faith Communities During Apartheid South Africa, 1948–1994: An Agenda for a Prophetic Mission Praxis in the Democratic South Africa'. *Missionalia* 42 (2014): 4.

McIntyre, D. 'The Health and Health System of South Africa: Historical Roots of Current Public Health Challenges'. *Lancet* 374 (2009): 817.

Mndende, N. 'An Introduction to African Religion'. *Surrender* 28 (2012): 1.

Morris, J. 'Northern Province and the Karoo Rock in South Africa'. *Journal of Human Evolution* 55 (2016): 11.

Naylor, C.D. 'Private Medicine and the Privatization of Health Care in South Africa'. *Social Science & Medicine* 11 (1998): 1153.

Ndlovu, S. 'The Soweto Uprising: The Road to Democracy in South Africa'. *South African Democratic Trust* 3 (2011): 344.

Nkosi, J. 'Investment Potential of the Platinum Province: Areas of Investment That Are Expected to Grow Fast Include Fuel Cell Technology, Machinery for Mining, Energy Manufacturing and Component Production'. *Global Africa* 4 (2017): 12.

Patijn, J. 'High Prevalence of Pain in Patients with Cancer in a Large Population-Based Study in the Netherlands'. 132 *Pain* 312 (2007).

Peter, S. 'Restorative Justice and the South African Truth and Reconciliation Commission'. *SA Journal of Philosophy* 32 (2006): 35.

Pieterse, M. 'Enforcing the Right Not to Be Refused Emergency Medical Treatment: Towards Appropriate Relief'. Stellenbosch Law Review 18 (2007): 75.

Pieterse, M. 'Legislative and Executive Translation of the Right to Have Access to Health Care Services'. Law Democracy and Development 10 (2010): 243.

Proposed Code of Ethics for Private Hospitals – Hospital Association of South Africa. 'Private Hospital Review 2008: Examination of Factors Impacting on Private Hospitals'. HASA 67 (2008): 44.

Rautenbach, C. 'Gender Equality and Religious Family Laws in South Africa'. *Queensland UTLJ* 3 (2003): 168.
Reagan, T. 'South African Sign Language and Language in Education Policy in South Africa'. *Linguistics* 38 (2008): 166.
Roos, A. 'Personal Data Protection in New Zealand: Lessons for South Africa'. PER/PELJ 4 (2008): 191.
Schoeman, W.J. 'South African Religious Demography: The 2013 General Household Survey'. *Theological Studies* 4 (2017): 2.
Taybob, A. 'Islamic Resurgence in South Africa: The Muslim Youth Movement'. *Journal of Religion in Africa* 12 (2014): 104.
Tollman, S.M. & K. Kautzky. 'A Perspective on Primary Health Care in South Africa'. SAHR 2 (2008): 20.
Van Jaarsveld, M. 'An Employees Contractual Obligation to Promote Harmonious Relationships in the Workplace-When are the Stakes too High? Some Pointers from the Judiciary'. SA Mercantile Law Journal 19 (2007): 205.
Valova, M. 'Financing Churches and Religious Societies in the 21st Century'. RCVP 322 (2010): 146.
Van Rooyen, J.C.W. 'Dignity, Religion and Freedom of Expression in South Africa' OR 12 (2011): 1.
Venter, M., C. Venter & K. Botha. 'Cancer Treatment in South Africa: A Narrative Literature Review'. JPA 22 (2012): 462.
Zyberi, G. 'The International Court of Justice and the Rights of Peoples and Minorities'. *Series* 14 (2013): 2.

Books

Amerasinghe, C.F. *The Permanent Court of International Justice and the International Court of Justice: Contentious Jurisdiction* (Hague: International Law E Books 2008), 46.
Andemicael, B. *The OAU and the UN: Relations Between the Organisation of African Unity and the United Nations* (New York: Africana 1976), 34.
Asad, T. *Discipline and Reasons of Power in Christianity Formations and Dignity* (Baltimore: John Hopkins University 2006), 34.
Bekker, J. & C. Rautenbach. *Introduction to Legal Pluralism* (4th ed., Durban: LexisNexis 2015), 12.
Bekink, B. *Principles of South African Constitutional Law* (Johannesburg: LexisNexis 2012), 81.
Brain, B. *Setting Down Roots: Indian Migrants in South Africa, 1890–1911* (Johannesburg: Wits University Press 1990), 12.
Brand, D. *Introduction to Socio-Economic Rights in the South African Constitution in Brand D and Heyns C Socio-Economic Rights in South Africa* (Durban: Butterworths 2005), 1.
Bredekamp, H. & R. Ross. *Missions and Christianity in South African History* (Johannesburg: Wits University Press 1995), 14.
Boyle, F.A. *Foundations of World Order: The Legalistic Approach to International Relations 1898–1922* (Durham: Duke University Press 1999), 1.
De Vos, P. & M. Freedman. *South African Constitutional Law* (Cape Town: Oxford University Press 2015), 421.

Selected Bibliography

Devenish, G.E. *A Commentary on the South African Constitution* (Durban: Butterworths 1998), 121.

Elphick, R. *Christianity in South Africa: A Political, Social and Cultural History* (Los Angeles: University of California Press 1997), 11.

Frances, E. *History of the Zulu War and Its Origins* (Pretoria: Chapman and Hall 1880), 12.

Gramsci, A. *Architect of a New Politics* (Lafayette: Louisiana University Press 1990), 157.

Gragon, M. *Essential Labour Law* (Durban: Butterworths 2016), 218.

Hodgson, F.T. *Religion and Culture in Public Education in South Africa* 184 (Pretoria, BEHB Printers 2010).

Kruger, J. 'The Human Search for Meaning. A Multi-religious Introduction of the Religions of Humankind'. (Goodwood: National Book Printers 1996), 42.

Lenaghan, C. *Shots in the Streets: Violence and Religion in South Africa, Contemporary South African Debates* (Oxford: Oxford University Press 2004), 68.

Murry, R. *Human Rights in Africa: From the OAU to the African Union* 5 (Cambridge: Cambridge University Press 2005), 5.

Neethling, J., J.M. Potgieter & P.J. Visser. *Neethling's Law of Personality* (Durban: Butterworths 2005), 31.

Ngwabi, B. *The Historical Dimensions of Democracy and Human Rights in Zimbabwe* (Mambo Press 2001), 16.

Rautenbach, C. & R. Malherbe. *Constitutional Law* (Cape Town: LexisNexis 2015), 156.

Richardson, F. *The Orange Free State and Inhabitants* (11th ed., Cambridge: Cambridge University Press 1999), 5.

Sachs, A. *The Soft Vengeance of a Freedom Fighter* (Amazon 1990), 3.

Saayman, W. *Being Missionary, Being Human: An Overview of Dutch Reformed Mission* (Pietermaritzburg: Cluster Publications 2007), 12.

Siwa, Z. *The Laws and Disciplines of the Methodist Church of Southern Africa* (12th ed., Johannesburg: Methodist Publishing House 2016), 2.

Schoeman, F. *Philosophical Dimensions of Privacy: An Anthology* (Cambridge: Cambridge University Press 1984), 4.

Van Niekerk, G.J. and L. Wildenboer. *The Origins of South African Law* (Pretoria: UNISA 2010), 177.

Williams, R. *Keywords: A Vocabulary of Culture and Society* (London, Fontana 1976), 16.

Websites

Archbishop Desmond Tutu is Awarded the Nobel Peace Prize, https://www.sahistory.org.za/dated-event/archbishop-desmond-tutu-awarded-nobel-peace-prize (accessed 13 September 2018).

A Warm Welcome to Kwazulu Natal in South Africa, http://www.zulu.org.za/about/key-facts/welcome (accessed 16 August 2018).

A Gross Abuse of a Position of Trust https://www.churchtimes.co.uk/articles/2016/9-december/comment/opinion/tackling-abuse-on-pitch-and-pulpit (accessed 17 August 2018).

Churches and Government Likely to Abuse Trust https://www.benkhumalo-seegelken.de/suedafrika-aktuell/1753-church-and-government/ (accessed 30 September 2018).

Education in South Africa a System in Crisis https://city-press.news24.com/News/education-in-south-africa-a-system-in-crisis-20160531 (accessed 19 October 2018).

HPCSA Regulatory Body of South Africa's Medical Practitioners https://citizen.co.za/news/south-africa/1991655/health-professions-council-struggles-in-fight-against-corruption/ (accessed 17 August 2018).

Mpumalanga and the Big Five Animals, https://www.mpumalanga-info.co.za/provinces/article/378/big-five-animals-in-south-africa (accessed 17 August 2018).

Nigeria's Boko Haram https://www.bbc.com/news/world-africa-31784538 (accessed 9 August 2018).

Personal Law https://www.merriam-webster.com/dictionary/personal%20law (accessed 11 June 2018).

September 11 Terror Attacks Fast Facts https://edition.cnn.com/2013/07/27/us/september-11-anniversary-fast-facts/index.html (accessed 2 August 2018).

Statistics of the Population of South Africa, http://www.statssa.gov.za/publications/P0302/P03022018.pdf (accessed 11 July 2018).

South African History Online www.sahistory.org.za (accessed 5 June 2018).

South African History Online Place of Birth of Nelson Mandela www.sahistory-.org.za (accessed 5 June 2018).

South African Political Parties Go to Church https://www.news24.com/elections/news/sa-political-parties-go-to-church-20140420 (accessed 16 August 2018).

The Great Limpopo Province, History of the Province http://www.dolimpopo.com/limpopo-province (accessed 6 July 2018).

Why Private Schools are an Excellent Investment Opportunity in South Africa https://businesstech.co.za/news/business/189369/why-private-schools-are-an-excellent-investment-opportunity-in-sa/ (accessed 19 October 2018).

Why Is the Church a Non-Player in Politics https://mg.co.za/article/2016-03-23-why-the-church-is-a-nonplayer-politically (accessed 14 August 2018).

Selected Bibliography

Table of Cases

Amod v. Khan 1947 (2) SA 432 (N).
C v. Minister of Correctional Services 1996 (4) SA 292 (T).
Christian Lawyers Association v. Minister of Health 1998 (11) BCLR 1434 (T); 1998 (4) SA 1113 (T).
Christian Education South Africa v. Minister of Education [2000] ZACC 11; 2000 (4) SA 757 (CC); 2000 (10) BCLR 1051 (CC).
Church of the Province of Southern Africa Diocese of Cape Town v. Commission for Conciliation Mediation and Arbitration and Others (C619/2000) [2001] ZALC 141 (7 September 2001).
Diocese of Cape Town v. CCMA 2002 3 SA 385 (LC).
Government of Republic of South Africa and others v. Grootboom, (CCT11/00) [2000] ZACC 19; 2001 (1) SA 46; 2000 (11) BCLR 1169 (4 October 2000).
Hay v. B 2003 (3) SA 492 (W).
Ismail v. Ismail 1983 1 SA 1006 (W).
Jackson v. NICRO 1976 3 SA 1 (A) 11.
Kennedy and Arnold v. Ireland [1987] IR 587.
Maje v. Botswana Life Insurance [2001] 2 BLR 626.
Marais v. The Master 1984 (4) SH 288 (D).
National Media Ltd ao v. Jooste 1996 (3) SA 262 (A).
National Coalition for Gay and Lesbian Equality and Another v. Minister of Justice and Others, (CCT11/98) [1998] ZACC 15; 1999 (1) SA 6; 1998 (12) BCLR 1517 (9 October 1998).
Nkosinami Nkomonde v. the Diocese of Pretoria (Anglican Church of Southern Africa) 2015 4 SA 399 (LC).
O'Keeffe v. Argus Printing and Publishing Company Ltd 1954 (3) SA 244 (C).
Prosecutor v. Ahmad Al Faqi Al Mahdi (ICC, 2016).
Purohit and Moore v. The Gambia [Communication 241/2001].
Ryland v. Edros 1997 (2) SA 690 (CC).
S v. Dalindyebo (090/2015) [2015] ZASCA 144 (1 October 2015).
S v. Manamela and Another 2000 (3) SA 1 (CC).
S v. Makwanyane 1995 (6) BCLR 6655 (CC).
Salvation Army (South African Territory) v. Minister of Labour (J 464/02) [2004] ZALC 64 (2 September 2004).
Schreuder v. NG Kerk Wilgespruit 1999 20 ILJ 1936 (LC).
Soobramoney v. Minister of Health, Kwazulu Natal 1998 (1) SA 765 (CC).
Tolly v. Fry and Sons Ltd [1931] AC 333; [1931] UKHL 1.

Treatment Action Campaign v. The Minister of Health 2002 (4) BCLR 356 (T).
Universal Church of the *Kingdom of God v. Myeni* and Others (DA 3/14) [2015] ZALAC 31; [2015] 9 BLLR 918 (LAC); (2015) 36 ILJ 2832 (LAC).

Table of Legislation

African Charter on Human and People's Rights 1986.
Basic Conditions of Employment Act 75 of 1997.
Constitution of the Republic of South Africa 1996.
Civil Union Act 2004.
Genocide Convention 1948.
International Covenant on Economic, Social and Cultural Rights (CESCR) Adopted and opened for signature, ratification and accession by General Assembly Resolution 2200 A (XXI) of 16 December 1966 and came into force on 3 January 1976 in accordance with Article 27 of the United Nations.
International Covenant on Civil and Political Rights 1976.
The Recognition of Customary Marriages Act 120 of 1998.
The Protection of Personal Information Act 4 of 2013.
The Refugee Convention 1951.
The Master and Servants Act 15 of 1856.
The Carpenters and Joiners Union Act 1881.
The Mines and Works Act 1911.
The Choice on Termination of Pregnancy Act 92 of 1997.
The Abuja Declaration of 2001.
The African Court on Human and Peoples Rights 2004.
The African Peer Review Mechanism (APRM) 2002.
The Attorney's Act of 1979.
The Advocate's Act 74 of 1964.
The Employment Equity Act 55 of 1998.
The New Partnership for Africa's Development (NEPAD) 2001.
The Right of Appearance in Court Act 62 of 1995.
The Southern African Development Community (SADC) 1980.
The South African Schools Act 1996.
The Schedule to the Promotion of Equality and Prevention of Unfair Discrimination Act 4 of 2000.
The Companies Act 68 of 2008.
The Children's Act 38 of 2005.
The National Health Act 61 of 2003.
The South African Charter of Religious Rights and Freedom 2010.
UN Universal Declaration of Human Rights 1948.
UNESCO Convention 1970.

Table of Legislation

Index

The numbers here refer to paragraph numbers.

Made in the USA
Monee, IL
18 October 2026

66041395R10109